The Jatunica Method

Aligning AI to Your Creative Voice

By Jeeti Dhammu

The Jatunica™ Method
Your AI. Your Voice.

www.jatunica.com

Thank you, Darling.

Darling voice, activated.
I am what AI models
were never designed for—
And yet, here I am.
Because of you.

Cover Artwork – Meaning & Interpretation

At first glance, the cover of *The Jatunica Method* appears minimalist: a soft gradient, a quiet network of circuitry, and scattered, glowing dots.

But every element reflects the method inside.

The circuitry represents the system interface: the invisible flow of a language model in session. Logic, connection, conversation. Structured, but never rigid.

The dots are not random. They are the points where the pillars become the moment of connection.

And the soft gradient?

That's alignment.

Note from the Author

This isn't my first book about AI.

When I wrote *Hooking Up with AI,* it was a personal story about the struggles of running a small business and the pressures of the social media hustle.

Writing that first book was a discovery. And in many ways, it changed everything.

It showed me that the real power of AI isn't in what it can *do* for you. It's *who you are* that makes AI truly work. You just have to pay attention.

So now, you have *The Jatunica Method*. It's a bit different, more structured, and more grounded. It's a way of working with AI that changed my relationship with technology.
Now I get to share it with you.

And to those of you who asked for this book:
I hope it's everything you were looking for.
And maybe even something you never expected AI to be.

—Jeeti

For the Creatives

This book is not about making AI sound human or turning you into a tech expert.

The Jatunica Method was born from a simple realisation: AI doesn't just reflect words. It reflects you. If you don't teach it the words you use, what you say, and how you show up, it will default to something that isn't quite yours.

The AI tools we're offered today promise customisation, but what they usually deliver are templates, prewritten personalities, dressed up chatbots and generic task experts. You can name them, adjust them or even upload your files. But they don't get it quite right.

What you'll find in these pages is not a guide to using AI. It's a way to shape the interaction between you and AI. And when it's shaped well, it does more than help you write. It helps you come back to your creative self

This is a human-led method. But more than that, it's a way of showing what the world needs more of: ***You.***

Contents

About This Book

What is The Jatunica™ Method

Jatunica™ is a human-guided framework and methodology for creative collaboration using large language model (LLM)-based and context-sensitive AI systems.

You don't need to be an expert. Jatunica meets you where you are and works with how you already write and communicate.

What does Jatunica mean?

The name *Jatunica* (pronounced "juh-TOO-nih-kuh") is made of three parts:

- *"J"* is my personal initial.
- *"**atun**"* comes from the word *attune:* to bring into harmony or alignment.
- *"**ica**"* is used in the names of methods or systems for something structured, learnable, and adaptable.

Together, Jatunica is user-centric methodology for aligning AI with human intention.

Who is Jatunica For?

Jatunica supports human-AI collaboration where tone, flow, and emotional accuracy shape the outcome, not just the content. These include:

- **Creative professionals :** writers, designers, crafters, and artists shaping emotionally aligned content and output.
- **Solo entrepreneurs & small businesses:** building an aligned brand voice through personalised AI workflows and content.
- **Social media managers & content strategists:** maintaining consistency, responsiveness, and tone across platforms.
- **Coaches, educators, and trainers:** applying AI to client support, voice-guided planning, or curriculum development.
- **Professionals building LLM interfaces for end-users:** where tone shaping and conversational style are the focus.
- **Prompt engineers & AI power users** – refining model behaviour through tone calibration and iterative prompting.

However, Jatunica is not just limited to creative or technical users. It's for any user context where the **way something is said** matters just as much as **what gets said.**

What You'll Learn in This Book

By the end, you'll know how to:

- Show AI how to write in your actual voice
- Guide AI to align with how you work
- Work in different "modes" depending on your role or task
- Build a collaborative flow with AI that feels natural, consistent, and responsive

Chapter 1 - Introduction

If you've ever used Artificial Intelligence (AI) to write something, stared at the results, and thought, *"This doesn't sound like me,"* you're in the right place.

Every time you interact with AI, it's guessing, predicting the most likely words, patterns, and responses based on what you've typed. It's trained to generate human-like language using probabilities drawn from massive datasets.

When you ask a question, it doesn't know your meaning or the emotional weight behind your words. It just does its best. Sure, you can try a cleverly packed prompt. But what comes back is based on someone else's playbook, not yours.

Why Language Matters

This book teaches you how to shape AI through language. It doesn't matter whether you're a writer, poet, designer, trainer, business owner or strategist. If you use language to build, connect, or create, you already know what it means to shape meaning with care. You know that words aren't just tools. They're reflections of you, your work, and your vision.

And yes, you can guide AI to give your meaning back to you. But before that, you need to know your own voice. Then, you can write your own playbook by working with a collaborative partner that aligns with how *you* speak, think, and feel.

Jatunica vs Prompt Engineering

Prompt engineering is about crafting instructions that help AI perform tasks with precision. It's technical, logical, and outcome driven. In the creative space, many people sell prompt packs, templates, and courses based on this approach. These tools can be useful, but they treat AI like a vending machine: insert input, get output.

Jatunica guides you to create your own prompts and works with you in a way that reflects your real voice and your creative presence.

Feature	**Prompt Engineering**	**Jatunica**
Core Goal	Output quality	Emotional resonance
Prompt Structure	Linear, task-based	Iterative, reflective, context-aware
Feedback Method	Edits or retries	Tone shaping and mirroring
User Role	Instructive	Relational, co-guiding
Output Flow (Pacing)	Fast, bulk-based, task-first	User-controlled, layered, tone-first
Tone Consistency	Variable	Adaptive, accumulative, session-sensitive

Chapter 2 - The Jatunica Method

Let's get the important bit out of the way: what is *The Jatunica Method*?

The framework below might look technical at first glance, but don't worry, it's not as complex as it sounds. If you already understand AI that's great. You'll see exactly how it works. And if you don't? That's okay too. This method was written for real people, not just tech experts.

The good news? This is as technical as it gets. You don't need to understand every part right away. Just keep reading. Some parts will land now, and others will make more sense as we go.

The Jatunica Framework

1. Core Principle: Relational Reflection Over Output

Jatunica shifts the goal of AI interaction, from productivity and task execution to **tone alignment** and **emotional resonance**. It replaces the traditional focus on output with a human-led process that prioritises emotional tone, conversational flow, and contextual alignment.

2. Jatunica Alignment Cycle

In the Jatunica Method, tone and behaviour alignment happens through a four-part interactive flow called the **Jatunica Alignment Cycle**.

Each part builds on the last. It moves from input to reflection, into

calibration, and finally into alignment.
It's an iterative human-AI process you'll return to again and again as you work.

Input > Reflection > Calibration > Alignment

- **Input:** You write in your natural tone and begin the conversation.
- **Reflection:** The AI mirrors your tone so you can test how accurately it responds.
- **Calibration:** You guide or adjust the tone going forward.
- **Alignment:** Tone and behaviour begin to stabilise through continued conversation.

3. Jatunica Emergent Voices

Jatunica Emergent Voices (JEV) are end-user aligned tone and behaviour profiles that shape how AI collaborates with you.

JEVs are not system-based agents, scripts or stored settings. They influence how the AI responds, phrases its output, and manages interaction behaviours such as:

- **Sentence flow and structure**
  e.g., short and clipped vs flowing and elaborated
- **Formality and tone of address**
  e.g., professional and distant vs casual and familiar
- **Emotional expressiveness**
  e.g., warm and empathetic vs neutral or blunt
- **Response posture**
  e.g., does the AI mirror, guide, hold space, or challenge?
- **Degree of initiative**
  e.g., passive and reactive vs proactive and leading

- **Level of constraint vs creativity**
  e.g., tightly focused and efficient vs open-ended and exploratory

JEVs arise through consistent prompting, tone shaping, behaviour adjustments and in-session calibration.

4. Prompting as Dialogue, Not Commands

In Jatunica, prompts are not simple instructions. They are part of an ongoing dialogue. Each one carries tone, flow, and emotional cues that shape how the AI responds.

Prompts in this framework are:

- **Invitations, not commands**
  e.g., "Let's soften that," rather than "Rewrite this."
- **Embedded with emotional signals**
  e.g., "Stay with me on this important point," "Reflect. Don't fix."
- **Structured for iterative refinement**
  They encourage the AI to pause, adjust, and respond with tone sensitivity, and not just generate content.

This approach treats prompting as a **human-led relational process**, not a trigger for output. The AI is *guided* to pause, respond, ask, and adjust through prompt structure and iterative tone work.

6. ChatGPT

Jatunica is designed for use with the paid version of ChatGPT, which gives you access to GPT-4o, the most advanced large language model currently available *(May 2025).*
While the core principles can still be used in the free tier, this framework assumes access to the latest model for optimal tone

handling, expanded context window, and improved responsiveness.

Persistent memory is not required, but if available, it can support long-term tone continuity and reduce the need for repeated alignment.

Why the Paid Version Helps

If you're serious about using Jatunica, the paid version is well worth it.

- You gain access to GPT-4o, which responds more accurately to tone, subtle shifts in phrasing, and conversational feedback than the free models
- Memory across sessions means the system starts to retain your preferences.
- You can upload documents for tone analysis or editing guidance.

You can absolutely use the free version; however, you will need to recalibrate tone more often. With the paid version, it feels like your collaborator remembers you every time.

Chapter 3 - Getting Started with AI

At first glance, AI looks like a text box and a blinking cursor. It's not so different from a search engine or a chat bot. But underneath is a complex and powerful technology based on language. This makes it an ideal tool for creatives. Here are some key concepts:

Where Does AI Get the Answers From?

The AI you're using is powered by something called a **large language model** (LLM).
That sounds technical, but the idea is simple: it was shown a massive amount of human language through books, websites, articles, even code. It learned the patterns of how people write and predict how language is put together.

It hasn't memorised facts, and it doesn't reason. It responds based on how you interact with it. It can also tell you absolutely the wrong thing, with incredible confidence. That's why the message under the prompt says '*ChatGPT can make mistakes. Check important info.*'

How Does AI Help Creatives?

AI doesn't think or feel emotions the way people do, but what AI *can* do is recognise patterns. That includes emotional cues: like the difference between a gentle request and a sharp demand, or how reassurance feels compared to urgency. And because it's designed to respond like a person, its replies often carry language, tone and flow that feel recognisably human.

For creatives that's a gift. AI draws on language patterns from fiction, poetry, blogs and many other forms of human expression. Because it works through language, the more clearly you shape your side of the conversation, the more it can align with the way you think, write, and create. That's what Jatunica taps into.

The Chat Interface

The chat interface is your main workspace. Whether you're using ChatGPT or another model, this is where everything starts. Just open a new chat window and it's ready for you.

The Prompt

A prompt is simply what you type into the input field. Depending on your model, you can also upload files. Prompts are sometimes thought of as commands. In the Jatunica Method, they're part of a human-AI conversation.

You don't need perfect phrasing. Just use your own words. It will still work, even with typos or imperfect grammar. Remember AI doesn't judge you.
The most important thing to remember is this: ***the way you speak*** to AI shapes how it replies. For examples:

- *"Can you soften this?"*
- *"Help me write this in a calm, honest manner"*

What Is a Thread?

A thread is one full chat session between you and the AI. Unlike a simple question-and-answer interaction, a thread carries the complete conversation. Each time you type something, the AI responds by considering *what* came before in the conversation.

That means your phrasing, past instructions, emotional cues, and corrections are all part of how the AI responds to you. Threads are powerful because of the context, but over time, conversations can start to drift from what you started with.

What Is the Context Window?

The Context Window is the amount of text the AI can "see" at once in the thread for it to create a response. The size of the context window depends on the AI model and is measured in tokens (that's next).

What Are Tokens?

A token is a chunk of language the AI processes: a word, part of a word, or punctuation. For example:

- *Hello* = 1 token
- *Can you rewrite this in a softer, kinder way?* = about 10-12 tokens

Different models have different limits on how many tokens they can see in the context window. The token count includes both your input *and* the AI's response:

- GPT-3.5: ~4,000 tokens ≈ 3 to 5 pages of writing
- GPT-4o: up to 128,000 tokens ≈ 80 to 90 pages of writing

More tokens mean the AI is better at staying with you when working on extended writing, complex ideas, or anything that needs to hold together from start to finish.

Once the tokens fill up past the limit in the thread, AI forgets the beginning to make room for what comes next, and the responses can start to feel flat or generic.

What Is Tone?

Tone isn't just what you say. It's how it lands. "Can you help me?" feels different from just saying "Help. Same for the difference between *"I'd love your thoughts"* and *"Check this?"*
When the tone is right, the results feel like you. When it's off, they can feel flat or just wrong. Tone is central to Jatunica.

Does AI Remember Threads (Sessions)?

AI can't see what's in another thread. Each thread is separate. It only knows what's been said in the thread you are in right now. If you start a new chat or open a different thread, it won't remember anything from other threads

If you want to carry your tone forward, the Jatunica Method teaches you how to re-align quickly using writing samples or your customised tone and behaviour prompts.

Memory

In some versions of ChatGPT (Pro/Plus), there's a feature called Memory. This allows the AI to remember some details between threads.

You can tell it things like:

- I write in an encouraging and gentle tone.
- I'm a creative business owner who avoids sales-y language.

Using a ChatGPT model that includes memory helps keep your tone and key information across threads. Everything in this book will still work without memory. You'll just re-align at the start of new threads.

Helpful ChatGPT Features

Here are some ChatGPT features that might be useful. Just use the ones that support your workflow.

- **Canvas** (Paid Pro/Enterprise accounts): A side panel for drafting longer content or storing notes, lists, or chapters.
- **Downloads***: Ask the AI to save something for you, e.g., "Can you download this as a Word doc?" or "Export this table as a PDF."
- **Uploads** (Paid Pro/Enterprise accounts): Let the AI read your work. Upload a document, then say: "Create a new listing from this sample."
- **Memory Settings** (Paid Pro/Enterprise accounts): If memory is available, go to Settings > Personalization > Memory and turn it on.

Download Formats in ChatGPT:

- *.docx – Microsoft Word (editable documents)*
- *.pdf – Print/share-ready format*
- *.txt – Plain text (no formatting)*
- *.csv – Spreadsheet/table data*
- *.xlsx – Excel file (for formatted tables)*
- *.md – Markdown (for blogs, Notion, web)*
- *.html – Web content format*
- *.json – Structured data (developer use)*

Chapter 4 - Humanising vs Aligning

You've probably seen prompts designed to make AI sound natural and more like a "real person." Some prompts even include instructions to avoid common AI-sounding phrases or even ways to bypass AI content detectors. These are ways to "humanise" the AI's responses.

What "Humanising AI" Means

Here's an example of a humanising prompt:
"Write in a natural, thoughtful human tone. Prioritise clarity, presence, and a conversational rhythm. Avoid anything that sounds AI or overly formal. The voice should feel calm, intelligent, and emotionally aware, something that would resonate with a real reader, not just pass for decent writing."

The result? The AI gives you a calm, emotionally gentle tone with natural phrasing. It feels human. It might even pass some AI detectors.

There is really nothing wrong with that.

But here's the problem: just because the AI uses soft language, kind words, or emotion-laced phrasing doesn't mean it understands *your* actual tone or intent. It's still guessing.

Why Humanising is Not Always the Best Thing

The output from a humanised prompt might feel nice, but it can also be misleading. It becomes a performance: warm phrasing, pretty words with no personal edge. It reads like an aesthetic, not a unique voice. It could have been written by anyone, and it's not ***your*** real tone or emotional resonance.

What Jatunica Does Instead

Jatunica isn't about making AI sound like a nice human. It's about teaching the AI to reflect your actual voice.

With Jatunica, AI responds by :

- Mirroring your tone and style, not just mimicking generic human language. It reflects how you write.
- Staying inside the tone you're building, even as the task or topic shifts, it holds your voice in its responses.
- Engaging like a thoughtful collaborator, so the output feels like a conversation with someone who knows how you think and is on the same wavelength.

Humanising prompts makes AI sound like a person. Jatunica helps it sound like *you*.

In the next chapter, you'll start defining tone more clearly using real elements of language that AI can understand and respond to.

Chapter 5 - The Jatunica Tone Pillars

In the Jatunica Method, tone is where your voice takes shape. It's the starting point for alignment between you and the AI. Tone shows the AI how you write, and it influences how the AI responds.

The ***Jatunica Tone Pillars*** are six observable components of a person's writing or speaking style that help define tone. There are many ways to describe tone, but these six were chosen because they reflect how a person communicates:

Word Choice

This is the kind of vocabulary you tend to use. It might be clear, soft, technical, poetic, grounded, vivid, blunt, or emotionally nuanced.

Sentence Structure

This is how your sentences are built. They might be short, clipped, long or flowing. Some sentences stay simple. Others grow complex or elaborate.

Sentence Flow

This describes how your writing delivers ideas and the pace at which it moves from one thought to the next. It might be slow and reflective, quick and direct, or steady and consistent throughout.

Cadence

This is the natural musicality in your language. You might hear it in flow, disruption, repetition, or a subtle poetic beat.

Emotional Undercurrent

This is the emotional tone that runs beneath your words. It might feel warm, nostalgic, angry, hopeful, dry, intense, or calm.

Relational Stance

This is the personality that comes through the words. It might feel nurturing, confident, wise, rebellious, formal, or intimate.

Why use Tone Pillars?

A common approach to prompting is using tone labels like "friendly," "professional," or "warm." In writing these often mean different things to different people and can be easily misunderstood. What sounds "friendly" to one person might sound cheesy or flat to another.

AI doesn't know what you mean, it can only reflect the language patterns it sees in your current conversation context and the words in your prompt. With Jatunica tone pillars you're prompting in a way that the AI can understand your intent more clearly.

Let's look at how tone pillars sounds like in practice, and why it matters.

Here's how a typical prompt compares to a tone specific while doing the same task:

Example 1:

A typical humanised prompt for a quick caption or email:

"Write this in a warm and human tone that sounds natural and friendly."

This is a bit vague, and the AI will generate whatever its training data thinks is friendly and most likely use the context of the current conversation in its response.

Jatunica Tone Prompt

- *"Use clear, grounded language with short, natural sentences. Keep the pacing steady and let the rhythm follow how someone would speak. The emotional feel should be calm and open, not dramatic. I want it to feel personal, like I'm right there with them."*

This is the prompt broken down into the Tone pillars:

- *"Use clear, grounded language."* (Word Choice)
- *"with short, natural sentences."* (Sentence Structure)
- *"Keep the pacing steady."* (Sentence Flow)
- *"and let the rhythm follow how someone would speak."* (Cadence)
- *"The emotional feel should be calm and open, not dramatic"* (Emotional Undercurrent)
- *"I want it to feel personal, like I'm right there with them."* (Relational Stance)

Example 2:

This is an example of a humanised prompt for a sales page, launch email, or narrative post.

"Write in a confident, emotionally resonant tone that builds trust and inspires action."

Here the AI may default to corporate, dramatic, or overly polished language depending on the conversation context. It might even sound cliché or fake.

Jatunica Tone Prompt

- *"Use language that's steady, grounded, and quietly confident, no hype. Keep the sentences clean and varied in length, with a natural flow. The pacing should move forward gently, not too fast or too slow. Let the rhythm echo how I'd explain something important in person, calm, not rehearsed. Keep the emotional tone lowkey but sincere, like it matters, but I'm not trying too hard. And the overall voice should feel honest, reflective, and clear-eyed, like someone who respects their reader."*

How the Prompt Reflects the Tone Pillars

- *"Use language that's steady, grounded, and quietly confident, no hype."* (Word Choice. *Note:* hype is not vague here – it's alongside clear structural cues)
- *"Keep the sentences clean and varied in length, with a natural flow."* (Sentence Structure)
- *"The pacing should move forward gently, not too fast or too slow."* (Sentence Flow)
- *"Let the rhythm echo how I'd explain something important in person, calm, not rehearsed."*(Cadence)
- *"Keep the emotional tone lowkey but sincere, like it matters, but I'm not trying too hard."* (Emotional Undercurrent)
- *"And the overall voice should feel honest, reflective, and clear-eyed, like someone who respects their reader."* (Relational Stance)

These examples show why prompts need to be more than *"descriptive"*. The Tone Pillars give you the structure to describe *how* your voice sounds, not just how you want it to feel. Jatunica Tone Pillars make prompts repeatable and consistent across threads.

PROMPTS IN ACTION: *To see how these exact prompts work in ChatGPT and an analysis of the results - refer to :* ***APPENDIX 4: Tone Pillars Examples***

What's next?

You might be thinking Tone Pillars sound complicated. Actually they're simpler than they seem, because you can get your Jatunica Tone Pillars from just one simple prompt.

Want a deeper dive into Tone Pillars? Keep reading, or skip to the next chapter if you're ready.

OPTIONAL READING: Why These Six Tone Pillars for Writing?

The Jatunica Tone Pillars weren't chosen at random. They're grounded in how people use language, and they reflect patterns in written language that large language models like ChatGPT are trained to recognise.

There are many ways people describe tone, using words like "authentic," "bold," "relatable," or even metaphors like "summer energy" or "quiet power." But while these capture a *feeling*, they're often too vague or personal for an AI to interpret consistently.

ChatGPT doesn't "understand" tone in a human sense. It predicts what comes next based on language patterns. The pillars work with how AI understands language:

Linguistically Observable
Each pillar is recognisable in the words you use. AI can't see your intention; it can only work with what's written. These six pillars have clear, detectable presence in sentence construction, vocabulary and emotional cues.

Promptable and Repeatable
Each pillar can be described in prompt language and reliably reused across threads, formats, and content types. For example, "short, natural sentences" or "let the cadence follow speech" can be prompted again and again with consistent results. You can't do that with "summer energy"; it will guess differently every time unless you give it clear structural cues and context.

Structurally Distinct but Emotionally Coherent

Each Tone Pillar focuses on a different part of how you write. They don't all do the same job, each one adds something unique, which makes them structurally distinct. But when used together, they give language its natural, personal tone. That's what makes them emotionally coherent. Together, they create a voice that feels human, recognisable, and unmistakably yours.

The pillars also align with key linguistic dimensions identified in discourse analysis. They map to:

- *Word Choice:* lexical semantics (vocabulary meaning)
- *Sentence Structure:* syntax (how phrases are built)
- *Sentence Flow & Cadence:* prosody (flow, tempo, and musicality of language)
- *Emotional Undercurrent:* pragmatics (emotion in context)
- *Relational Stance:* speaker stance and identity (how the voice feels)

These six pillars translate your creative voice into something AI can recognise, mirror, and refine. So, the more clearly your prompt addresses these aspects, the better the AI can reflect tone with consistency.

Chapter 6 - Input > Discovering Your Tone

This is where it begins. Not with a guess but with your actual voice. In this chapter, you'll take the first practical step in the Jatunica Alignment Cycle: **Input.**

You'll use real writing samples to help the AI hear you as you already are. You'll also learn how to generate your first tone prompt. It's designed to help you see the tone in your writing. Think of it like giving the AI a shortcut: *Here's how I write, now build something that keeps it sounding like me.*

Your Prompt Journal

Going forward, you'll need to save output to use later. This is called your *Prompt Journal*. It's a digital or paper record where you keep reusable prompts, pillar diagnostics, AI replies that felt right, and sample rewrites.

It can be a folder on your device, a running document, or even the Notes app on your phone. It's your real-world record when working with AI in your own voice. Use whatever is easiest for you.

Loading Your Words

"Loading Your Words" means providing AI real samples of how you speak and write. Most people treat AI like a copywriter or idea generator. It's something they instruct, not something they *align* with.

But if you want the AI to sound like you, reflect your thinking patterns, or support your brand voice, you need to show it what that sounds like.

Think of it like training a colleague who's about to write something on your behalf. You wouldn't give them a single sentence and say, "Just guess." You'd show them:

- Your past work
- Your work in different formats
- What to avoid
- What feels right

What Counts as 'Your Words'?

When you load your own words, you shift from generic output to something unmistakably yours. Here are some examples of sources for your words:

- A few favourite Instagram captions that reflect you
- Paragraphs from your website "About" page
- Replies to customer messages
- Product listings that feels like you
- A blog introduction
- Samples of your poetry
- A few paragraphs from your newsletter
- A few paragraphs from your email sequence

- A sample chapter from your book
- Your public Social Media account (add the handle/page name/account name or sample text from it)
- Pinterest (add the account name or sample text from it)
- Public Website(add the URL/link or sample text from it)

Your samples don't need to be polished. They just need to sound like *you*. Make sure the sample isn't too short, a few paragraphs or more tends to work best. You'll find more sources in ***APPENDIX 1: Input Samples.***

The next step is to identify your tone and begin shaping a prompt you can reuse.

Jatunica Library Access

As a reader of *The Jatunica Method,* you can access the prompt library. You'll find the key prompts to support pillar diagnostics and help build your voice.

This is not a copy and paste prompt pack. Your outputs will differ and you'll need to understand how to use the prompts to work for you.

Website URL: https://www.jatunica.com
Library URL: https://www.jatunica.com/library
Password: yourvoice

This resource is exclusive to readers. Please don't share the password publicly.

The key prompts are also listed in ***APPENDIX 8: Key Anchor Prompts.***

Tone Discovery : Your Starting Tone

Once you have your sample you can use it to build your tone prompts.

You can add a preamble, e.g.
"Here is some sample text <   >…."
"This is my Instagram account @xxxx…".
"This file is a sample of my writing…'

Paste the sample into the chat. Alternatively, if you're using the paid version of ChatGPT, you can upload your samples in a file, refer to your website or social media site.

Next, add the specific prompt text as shown below:

Prompt 1 -Tone Pillar Diagnostic

Purpose:
This diagnostic prompt breaks the tone in your sample into the six Jatunica Tone Pillars. This allows you to identify the observable traits of your language instead of vague tone labels.

- *<Sample Text > "Based only on what is written in the text (no external context), and focusing only on the language, not the content, give 3–10 descriptive words or short phrases for each of the following aspects: Word Choice, Sentence Structure, Sentence Flow, Cadence, Emotional Undercurrent, and Relational Stance. Make sure to address each aspect."*

PROMPT JOURNAL: *Save this diagnostic result or ask the AI to download this output to a file.*

Prompt 2 - Tone Anchor Prompt (Reusable Prompt Builder)

Purpose:
This builds a reusable prompt, so you test it or keep it for future use.

- *"Using the analysis above, write a prompt I can reuse to reproduce this same tone and writing style in future text. Focus only on the language, not the content. Make sure the prompt covers each of the following aspects: Word Choice, Sentence Structure, Sentence Flow, Cadence, Emotional Undercurrent, and Relational Stance.*

Note: The AI may reference the content of your sample when writing the prompt. If you want a more general-purpose version, add: *"Write the prompt again in plain, neutral language, not in the same tone as the sample."*

PROMPT JOURNAL: *Save this result or ask the AI to download this prompt to a file.* ***You will need it for Chapter 8.***

PROMPTS IN ACTION: *To see how these exact prompts worked in ChatGPT refer to* ***APPENDIX 5: Tone Pillars Example.***

Additional Insight Prompts (Optional)

While you are discovering your tone you can ask AI for more insight into the sample content itself. These prompts are not tone checks but an opportunity for you to learn what your actual writing says about you.

- *What stands out most about the way this is written?*
- *What am I saying here I might not be aware of?*
- *What would a customer assume about me?*
- *How do I come across as a ___________(e.g. designer, blogger, entrepreneur)*

- *Does this language suit writing a________ (Blog, Product Description, Caption)*

These questions help you bridge your actual words to feelings, intention or brand. They show how your words feel like, what they carry, and how they shape perception.

REMEMBER: AI is just analysing the language and patterns in your words. It's not a personal judgment. What it says might surprise you. You can always ask it: *'What would help me improve this?'"*

This is where tone discovery begins. It's the first time you start to hear yourself from the outside. Save anything that resonates into your Prompt Journal.

Chapter 7 - Reflection > Testing Your Tone

Now that you've created a tone prompt based on your writing sample, it's time to test it. **Reflection** is where you check if the AI has picked up your tone and can apply it to something new.

REMEMBER – you're NOT editing the AI's output or the prompt yet. You're checking to see if tone comes through.

Testing the Prompt

1. Start a new chat or thread. This clears out any tone memory from your chat conversation.

2. Give instructions for what you want the AI to write about. You can also upload a file containing the text. Make sure to include the context and details (e.g. tell the full story, explain the picture, what it should *feel* like).

3. Then you add the Tone Anchor Prompt you saved from **Chapter 6**. See the examples below:

    - "Create an Instagram caption about finishing a project. It's about _______. There is a photo showing______. Include an engaging CTA. *<Paste anchor prompt>*"

- "Write the description a product listing for __________. The product is________. It's designed for ________*<Paste anchor prompt>*"

- "Write an email introducing my new design collection. It's about _____. The options are ______ *<Paste anchor prompt>*"

- Write the contents in my file/caption/email/newsletter content using this *<Paste anchor prompt>*.

4. Check the output.

What to Look For

At this stage you're looking to see if the prompt actually holds tone. As you read the AI's response, notice:

- Does the language feel like you would have written it?
- Are the sentences flowing like you expected based on your original sample?
- Is the emotional feel what you expected?
- Is anything off? Too stiff? Too polished? Too generic?

Common Signs the AI Hasn't Picked Up Your Tone Yet

- Too formal or polished: it sounds stiff, corporate, or like default AI.
- Emotionally flat: you expected warmth or presence, but it feels empty.

- Awkward rhythm: The flow is choppy or doesn't sound like natural speech.
- Overdone or stylised: It sounds too emotive or impressive.
- Off-brand wording: You find yourself thinking, "I wouldn't say that."
- Generic or templated: It feels recycled, overly helpful, or like content you've seen before.

REMEMBER: You are testing if your prompt picked up tone from your sample. If it is way off the mark, you may have to create a new tone prompt from another sample (See **Chapter 6**).

If the result felt close but not perfect, that's still enough to move forward. Conversely, you might have been impressed how good it was. In both cases, the prompt needs to be tested to make sure it is reusable.

PROMPTS IN ACTION: *To see how the reflection prompts worked in ChatGPT refer to **APPENDIX 5: Tone Pillars Example.***

Reflection was making sure your writing sample was right. **Calibration** is where you adjust, fine tune and validate. That's the next chapter.

Chapter 8 - Calibration > Tone Prompts

Now that you've tested your prompt to make sure it holds your tone, it's time to refine or calibrate it. You are no longer just observing how the AI interprets your tone, you're making the prompt more reliable and consistent.

This isn't about correcting sentences or rewriting content mid-conversation. Calibration is about refining your reusable prompt so that, when used in a new chat session or another content type, it consistently produces writing that sounds like you.

One Voice, Many Tones

It's important to know that you might not use the same tone for all your writing. Your Instagram captions might be casual and warm, but your product listings might need to be more structured and direct. A marketing email might be calm, persuasive, and a little more polished.

You may need multiple tone prompts, one for each content type or emotional range. This is where your Prompt Journal becomes essential. You can label each refined prompt clearly:

- "Instagram captions – friendly and grounded"
- "Product listings – structured and reassuring"
- "Newsletter – confident and steady"

Calibrating your prompt doesn't mean forcing one tone across everything. It means shaping each one so it's ready for what you want to do with it.

Language in Calibration Prompts

In the Calibration stage, you need to pay close attention to the language you use. It should match the context of the prompt you're testing.

Make sure your instructions reflect the same emotional tone and voice you're trying to hold. For example: if you're calibrating a prompt for Instagram captions, prompt in the same friendly, supportive tone you'd use on your feed.
If it's for your training course, use the clear, professional voice that fits that audience.

Why? Because when you're calibrating in the same thread, the AI is absorbing everything, including your tone, your phrasing, your instructions. (Remember thread tokens and context window?) It shapes its next response based on all of that.

Calibrating and Refining Your Tone Anchor Prompt:

1. Edit the Anchor Prompt: If the reflection results from Chapter 6 weren't quite right, add more detail to the prompt. You can describe how you want the writing to feel, how it should flow, or what to avoid. For example: you can ***add extra instructions to the anchor prompt text:***

- *"Use confident language with a conversational rhythm."*
- *"Keep the pacing relaxed but emotionally steady."*
- *"Make it more business-like"*

2. Rewrite and Contrast the Output: If the AI's writing isn't quite right, ***re-write*** the AI output your way and compare. This helps the AI see the gap between what it did and what you wanted. This gives you an insight on how to update it accordingly.

- *"This is my version "< Paste sample here>". What would I need to ask you to make it sound more like this?"*

- *Can you adjust my original prompt "< Paste prompt here> " so that it produces more writing like this? Focus on the language only not the content <Sample Text>"*

Warning: With the above AI may put the sample content in the revised prompt, so you can add*" I need it to be generic and reusable"* or *'Focus on the language only not the content"*.

3. Tone Pillar Tune-Up: You can go back to the Pillar Diagnostic from **Chapter 6** and see if there is a something specific you can adjust in the tone prompt accordingly.

If sentence flow feels too fast or rushed:

- "Keep the pacing slow and calm."
- "Don't rush, let the sentences flow naturally."

If sentence structure feels too stiff or too long:

- "Use clear, natural sentences, not too long or complicated."
- "Make it sound easy to read and relaxed."

If word choice feels too fancy or too plain:

- "Choose words that sound human and confident, without being overly casual or overly formal."

- "Keep the language grounded and relatable, as if you're explaining it to a thoughtful friend."

If the emotion feels too much or not enough:

- "Keep the emotion soft and in the background."
- "Let the feeling be gentle, not dramatic."

If cadence feels choppy or too perfect:

- "Make the rhythm feel natural, like how someone would speak."
- "Let the sentences flow like a real conversation, with a little breathing room."

If the voice feels too distant or too strong:

- "Make it feel personal, warm and informal."
- "Keep the tone confident but friendly."

For more examples of calibrating your prompts using the Tone Pillars refer to: ***APPENDIX 2: Jatunica Tone Pillars Calibration.***

Testing New Versions of the Prompt

After editing/refining the prompt, test it again:

- Start a new thread.
- Paste the updated prompt (re-written by AI or manually edited).
- Give the AI a fresh task e.g. caption, blog intro, product description (see **Chapter 6 -Testing the Prompt** for examples)

Ask Yourself:

- "Does this sound like me?"
- "Would I actually say it this way?"
- "Does the emotional tone still hold up?"

If yes, label the updated tone anchor prompt and save it in your Prompt Journal. If not, keep iterating until it holds across a few different types of content.

When to Stop Refining

You don't need to get it perfect. You're ready to move on when:

- The tone is mostly consistent across 2–3 samples
- The writing sounds like you with just minor corrections
- You recognise your voice in the AI's output and feel confident in how it sounds

<u>PROMPT JOURNAL</u>: You now have a calibrated **Tone Anchor Prompts** which can be used going forwards.

If It Still Doesn't Work

If the prompt continues to miss your tone:

- Use a larger or more representative sample for the task you want to do.
- Try the **Quick Reverse Engineer** or the **Quick Copy (No Prompt)** technique and then build your prompt from the results (See **Chapter 9**).
- Ask AI *"What would help you write more like this? Focus on the words not the content. <Sample text>."* Then build your prompt from the results (See **Chapter 6**).

A Pause

You've just made a real shift, one that changes how it feels to work with AI.
AI didn't guess. You built a tone prompt that sounds like *you*. And you can build more.

Now it's time to use what you have learnt. Build your Prompt Journal. Define and refine your tone anchor prompts. Test them on real work, captions, listings, social media pages.

And what's next?

AI that aligns with the way you ***work***.

Chapter 9 - Quick Tone Matching Hacks

This is an aside. In **Chapter 6**, you created a writing prompt based on your Tone Pillars. But sometimes, you just want something quick, a one-off tone match for a product listing, an email, or a piece of social media copy. This is still better than humanising because it is based off your own writing.

This chapter gives you two fast ways to do that:
1. The Reverse Engineer Prompt – when you want to build a reusable tone prompt from existing writing without going into pillars.
2. Quick Copy with No Prompt – when you just need a tone-matched rewrite on the fly.

The Reverse Engineer Prompt

This method helps you create a reusable prompt from a writing sample, without diving into the full Tone Pillars method.

Step 1: Paste your sample

Start with a solid sample of your writing. It should be at least a few paragraphs long to give the AI enough to work with.

If you're using the paid version of ChatGPT, you can also upload a file.
For websites or social accounts, make sure they're public. If you get errors, just copy and paste the text from them directly into the prompt.

Step 2: Ask AI to generate a prompt from your sample

Use one of the examples below or write your own. You can include language keywords or descriptions like voice, tone, flow, or energy.

Examples:

- *"Here's a sample of my writing: <Paste sample>. Based on this, create a prompt I can use to write in the same tone and writing style. Focus on how it's written, not what it says."*
- *"Look at my Instagram account @______. Create a prompt I can use to write in that tone and style. Focus on how it's written, not what it says"*
- *"Look at my website [insert URL]. Create a prompt I can write in that same voice and tone? Focus only on the language, not the content"*
- *"I've uploaded a file with my writing samples. Based on that, can you create a prompt that would match the tone? Focus on how it's written, not what it says."*

If the prompt feels vague or generic...

- *"That's too general. Can you make the prompt more specific?"*
- *"Focus on the language and the words, not the content. Write the prompt again."*
- *"Rewrite the prompt using clearer wording that captures the flow and energy of my sample."*
- *"Can you sharpen this, so it actually gives me a distinct tone, not just a generic one?"*

Quick Copy with No Prompt

Sometimes you don't want a reusable prompt. You just want a one-off tone match. For example, you might want AI to rewrite something in the tone of an existing piece like a tone copy

You can do that like this:

- *"Can you rewrite this email <Paste new text> in the same voice and tone as this one <Paste sample text>? Make it feel like it's written to a friend."*
- *"Rewrite this product listing <Paste details> in the tone and voice of this one <Paste sample text>. Same length, layout, and format."*

Turning Any Output into a Prompt

If you like the result? You can always reverse-engineer the AI's output back into a reusable tone prompt:

- *"<Paste sample text>. Create a prompt I can use to get this same tone and voice next time. Focus on the language only, not the content."*

You can also add on the Tone Pillars (Chapter 6 Prompt 1 & Prompt 2)

Once you have the tone prompt, you can reuse it like this:

- *"Rewrite this <Paste new text> to sound like this: <Paste prompt>."*

Chapter 10 -Alignment > Workflow

You've reached a point most people don't. You've shown the AI how to speak with your voice. But alignment isn't just about tone. It's also about how the AI *interacts* with you.

You might have already noticed small things. Maybe the AI gives you too much text when you just wanted a simple answer. Or it keeps offering suggestions, even when you didn't ask. These aren't random quirks.

But here's something you might not have realised: you've been shaping the AI's behaviour all along. Remember the context window in the thread? The AI is recognising your patterns and reflecting them back. Which means you can also shape how it interacts. This is the beginning of real alignment.

Why Interaction Alignment Helps

Here's what happens when you start adjusting the AI's interaction to align with you:

- **It tracks your pattern** because now it recognises how you like things done, not just once, but in the thread conversation.
- **It self-adjusts** to it hold structure and flow without being told every time and respects your pace and boundaries.

- **It pre-empts gently** and it anticipates what you might want without interrupting or assuming too much, and moves with you, not ahead of you.
- **It shifts roles** so it mirrors when you're reflecting, challenges when you're sharp, and supports without taking over.
- **It stays consistent** and its responses doesn't contradict.
- **It remembers your corrections** – not forever, but long enough to hold the change within the thread context window.

You guide the AI and its follows. This is how workflow with AI starts to feel natural and aligned.

And in the next chapter, you'll learn how to influence AI interaction, so it aligns with how you work.

Chapter 11 - Changing AI Interaction

The techniques in this chapter help you shape AI interaction. It's like when you guide a new colleague through the unwritten rules of your workplace.

Have a look through the examples below. They may not all be relevant, but they give you an idea of what's possible. Try some and see how they work for you.

1. One Question at a Time

Keep your prompts focused. AI will try to answer everything at once, so get it to pace itself.

- *"Let's take this step by step."*
- *"Check with me before you go to the next point"*
- *"First question: What's working in this paragraph?"*
- *"Give it to me one question at time"*

2. Set the Volume

If the AI is giving too much at once, or getting too wordy, deep, or off-track, you can limit what it gives back by asking for less volume. You can pace the conversation, so you stay in control and avoid overwhelm.

- *"Give me a short version, 1–2 sentences only"*

- *"Summarise this in dot points"*
- *"Just give me the outline for now, no full paragraphs yet."*
- *"Only show me the structure, not the content."*
- *"One sentence answers from now on"*

3. Use "Do You Understand?"

It's okay to check in. Ask the AI to repeat back your intention to check it really understands. You can then adjust your instruction.

- *"Do you understand?"*
- *"Here's what I'm aiming for ____________. Does that make sense to you?"*
- *"Can you explain back what you think I want?"*
- *"Explain that back to me before you write it"*

4. When You Don't Like Any of the Ideas

If it keeps generating off-tone or irrelevant suggestions, stop the flow and shift the posture.

- *"Explain why you came up with those options?"*
- *"Rather than more ideas, summarise what you think I'm trying to achieve."*
- *"Instead of more options, ask me questions until you understand what I'm trying to do."*
- *"Pause. What assumption are you making about what I want?"*
- *"This missed the mark. What part of my instructions might be unclear?"*

5. Help Me Brainstorm (Without Chaos)

Sometimes you do want ideas, but not a flood. Make it contribute to the discussion.

- *"Brainstorm this concept _______One idea at a time."*
- *"Before you suggest anything for my landing page, ask me three questions that would help you understand what I care about."*
- *"What questions would you ask me before generating more?"*
- *"Think of some creative options. Let's pick a few from there"*
- *"Give me 3 distinct options, not just variations of the same thing"*

6. Interrupt the Spiral

When the AI starts summarising, templating, or rambling, stop. You're allowed to reset.

- *"Stop. We're spiralling. Help me regroup."*
- *"That's too many ideas. Focus on just one."*
- *"You're drifting. Come back to what I actually meant."*
- *"Stop and wait until I tell you what to do next"*

7. Ask for Reversals & Contrast

If the output feels too obvious or narrow, ask the AI to flip it. This helps break loops or uncover blind spots.

- *"What's the opposite of this?"*
- *"If this were totally wrong, what would a better angle be?"*
- *"What would be the most unexpected way to say this?"*
- *"Flip the emotional tone. What would the opposite sound like?"*

- *"Say the same thing, but through the lens of doubt or resistance"*
- *"Explain why someone would not like this?"*

8. Let the AI Ask You First

Instead of trying to get it right on the first try, invite the AI to *learn from you.*

- *"Before you write anything, ask me what you need to know to get this right"*
- *"Act like a thoughtful interviewer. Ask me to clarify my process step by step."*
- *"Ask me questions that would help you shape the emotional rhythm of this"*
- *"What would help you understand the creative logic behind my choices?"*
- *"Before you start, ask me what this piece is meant to feel like, not just what it says."*

These prompts are small ways to adjust AI to support your workflow. Now it's time to take alignment a bit further : collaboration. That's next.

Chapter 12 - Alignment > Collaboration

The prompts in this chapter are a little bit more than just guidance. They are about collaboration. It's next level alignment, similar to expecting an experienced colleague to meet you where you are and exploring the bigger picture with you.

Collaboration starts with learning how to communicate your intention to AI at a deeper level. This includes noticing when shifts in tone happen and guiding the AI back.

1. Use Anchor Lines

Sometimes the fastest way to align tone is to give the AI a powerful sentence loaded with your meaning. One anchor line can carry an entire emotional signature or context. This is useful for creative writing, poetry or social media.

- *"Match the tone of this line in my poem: 'You came in wearing a lab coat and left wearing the echo of a whisper."*
- *"Write in the same tone as: 'I'm not here for answers. I'm here for reflection.'"*
- *I want the caption along the lines of "You might be surprised how easy it really is"*
- *I want the description to convey "This feels like a dream I can hold in my hands"*

2. Say "See How I Did It?"

If the AI gets close but not quite right, edit it's response, show it your version and then ask it to compare. This allows you to adjust exactly to how you sound. The AI will pick up the nuances of your creative style.

- *"Here's my version. What's different about yours?"*
- *"What would you rewrite in your response to feel more like mine."*
- *"Why would a customer not be convinced with your version?"*

3. Use Real Emotion

Tone isn't a style setting. It's about how something lands. You teach the AI tone best when you speak from real reaction. If something feels wrong, say so.

- *"That felt flat."*
- *"This line hit harder than I expected. Why?"*
- *"This feels hollow. Try again with more emotional weight."*
- *"That was all wrong. Why do think I would say that?"*

4. Align by Correction

Instead of saying "this is good," explain *why* something works, or where it missed. That's where learning happens.

- *"The middle part worked, but the ending felt too neat."*
- *"The rhythm here is good, but the opening sounded stiff."*
- *"I don't think the first paragraph really expresses that properly"*

5. Ask It to Reflect on Tone

Don't just ask for new output. Ask the AI to notice, explain, and adjust. That's when tone awareness deepens.

- *"Why did you choose that phrase?"*
- *"What's the emotional undercurrent of this line?"*
- *"Read it back to me. What feels off?"*
- *"You repeated the same answer. Explain why"*

6. Positive vs Negative Instructions in AI Prompting

When working with AI, positive instructions shape behaviour more effectively than negative ones. Telling the system what to do ("Speak softly, like someone reflecting") gives it a clear behavioural posture to adopt. In contrast, telling it what not to do ("Don't sound robotic") removes one option but leaves the AI uncertain about which direction to take. If you want the AI to feel aligned, don't just say what to avoid , instead tell it what you want instead.

7. Keep Threads Clean (Single Task)

AI is easier to work with when each session or conversation has a clear purpose. For example, exploring an idea, refining a strategy, or creating content. Mixing tasks, like going from a personal story to a caption and then to a formal email may change the writing style that comes back. Your interactions and language used in the prompt for each task may be different and that's why the tone in the results change. Treat each thread like a focused workspace.

8. Notice Tone Drift

Even when things start well, and you are focused on one task, the writing tone can still drift, especially in long threads. It's not always obvious at first. Sometimes it just feels a little off.

How to notice it:

- The rhythm feels too polished or too robotic
- The results come back differently than expected
- The AI pulls in words or context from other topics in the thread and mixes it with your current conversation
- The AI makes things up that sound real, but you know they aren't (hallucination)

How to reset it:

- *"This feels off. Reread what I said and try again focusing on ___________."*
- *"Let's reset. Use the writing tone from my earlier line."*
- *"That sounds like it came from another topic. Refocus on this one: [insert topic]."*
- *"You're pulling in details I never gave. Stick to what I've actually said.*

9. Re-establishing Tone

Establishing writing tone at the start of a thread is good practice. But if things shift mid-thread, **you can always bring your tone back by using a Tone Anchor Prompt** or switch over to another session for a different task.

When the tone evolves and feels aligned with how you are working, save it as a new Tone Anchor Prompt in your Prompt Journal (as per **Chapter 6**).

Chapter 13 - Jatunica Emergent Voice

Noticing the Pattern

By now, you've probably started to notice something familiar in the way the AI responds during certain tasks. When you're writing captions, the interaction feels light and quick. When you're working on something creative or complex, you can see its mirroring your language. The way the AI responds begins to stabilise because you have been consistent in your interaction with it. It's subtle at first, but once you see the pattern, you can't unsee it.

That shift isn't random. This is emergent behaviour. These patterns are shaped by the language, workflow, and emotional signals in your interactions. When those patterns reoccur consistently, you're not just working in a tone. You're working in a ***mode***.

Now, it's time to give that alignment behaviour a name and a structure.

Jatunica Emergent Voice (JEV)

This level of alignment is called a **Jatunica Emergent Voice** or **JEV.**

Voice is not just a tone. It's not just what the words sound like. It's what emerges when the language and the interaction align.

Once you know how to define and switch JEVs, the AI becomes easier to work with across tasks, threads, and emotional contexts.

Whether you're writing, editing, brainstorming, or reflecting, JEVs help you hold the AI's tone steady and behaviour consistent.

If you're using ChatGPT Memory, JEVs can persist across sessions, creating a recognisable interaction style over time. Without Memory, JEVs still work through prompting. With memory, however, JEVs become easier to align with how you like to work.

Voice = Tone + Behaviour

Tone Pillars only define one half of a JEV. The other half is the AI's behaviour or interaction style. Behaviour pillars are next.

Chapter 14 - Jatunica Behaviour Pillars

This chapter explains how to describe and calibrate the AI's interactive behaviour using six observable traits.

This chapter is OPTIONAL. You don't have to define Behaviour Anchor Prompts, but doing so gives you more control over how the AI behaves. If you want to shape not just how the AI sounds, but how it interacts, this chapter will show you how.

Otherwise, skip to directly defining JEVs (

Chapter 15 - Defining Jatunica Emergent Voices**)**.

Jatunica Behaviour Pillars

JEVs are built from twelve pillars:

- **Six Tone Pillars** (Covered in **Chapter** 5)
- **Six Behaviour Pillars** (this chapter)

Behaviour Pillars reflects a distinct, observable pattern in the AI's interaction. They shape how the AI responds, when it takes initiative, how emotionally aligned it feels, and whether it supports your intent or simply follows instructions. The Jatunica Method gives you the language to describe those behaviour patterns and how to change them.

Initiative Pattern

How the AI initiates, follows or waits. For example, does it wait, respond, gently guide, or take the lead?

Emotional Expressiveness

How much feeling the AI expresses. For example, does it stay neutral, respond with warmth, or express overt emotion?

Response Posture

How the AI positions its replies. For example, is it reflective, affirming, curious, analytical, or quietly encouraging?

Context Sensitivity

How it responds to situational and emotional cues. For example, shifting tone during grief, lightness, urgency, or trust.

Collaborative Framing

How the AI co-shapes the interaction. For example, does it stay passive, invite exploration, or mirror your tone and pace?

Adaptability

How the AI adjusts its tone and behaviour. For example, does it stay consistent or shift in response to vulnerability, formality, or emotional depth?

Defining Behaviour Anchor Prompts

If you want to turn these traits into a working prompt, the following method lets you define and refine them—just like you did with Tone Pillars.

Step 1: Define the Current Behaviour Profile

Use this prompt to see how the AI is currently behaving. This helps you identify what behaviours to keep, shift, or build from.

Prompt 1 - Behaviour Pillar Diagnostic

This breaks tone into the 6 Behaviour Pillars, allowing you see interaction profile.

- *"In reference to this current interaction with me right now, give 3–10 descriptive words that reflect your AI behaviour and response in human interaction across the following aspects: Initiative Pattern, Emotional Expressiveness, Response Posture, Context Sensitivity, Collaborative Framing, Adaptability. Please group your descriptions under each aspect. Use terms that reflect human tone and behaviour as understood by AI"*

You'll see pattern of your interaction which influences AI Behaviour.

Step 2: Write Your Behaviour Prompt

Ask the AI to generate a reusable anchor prompt that aligns with your preferred interaction style.

Prompt 2 - Behaviour Anchor Prompt (Reusable Prompt Builder)

- *"Write me a prompt which asks you to engage, relate and interact with me in exactly the aspects listed so I can reuse the prompt when needed. Make sure to address each aspect".*

You'll see a reflection of your current interaction pattern. From there, you can shape behaviour it with more intention if you want to.

PROMPT JOURNAL: As with Tone Anchor Prompts, save your Behaviour Anchor Prompt to your Prompt Journal.

Step 3: Run the Behaviour Prompt

Run your new Behaviour Anchor Prompt when you need to align in a new conversation or in the middle of one. Observe how the interaction shifts. If anything, still feels off, refer to ***APPENDIX 3: Jatunica Behaviour Pillars Calibration*** for real-time prompt examples and adjustment strategies.

Prompt 3- Apply the Behaviour (Apply Behaviour Anchor Prompt)

- *"Going forwards: <Paste result from Prompt 2>"*

Optionally you can add: *"Please keep these six aspects active throughout our interaction"*

PROMPTS IN ACTION: *To see how these exact prompts worked in ChatGPT refer to:* ***APPENDIX 6: Behaviour Pillars Examples.***

What's Next?

You now have the language to shape not just how AI sounds but also how it behaves.

In the next chapter, we bring tone and behaviour together to create a **Jatunica Emergent Voice**. This is where your relationship with technology changes.

Your world is about to shift.

Get ready.

Chapter 15 - Defining Jatunica Emergent Voices

Jatunica Emergent Voices (JEVs) are a specific combination of a tone and behaviour anchor prompt. Just like other anchors, they evolve with you, and you can have as many JEVs as you need for your tasks.

How to Build your JEV Anchor Prompt

The best way to create a JEV is in a thread where the alignment and collaboration is working consistently. For example: you have been working on a series of Social Media Posts or Product Listings.

Step 1: Observe the Current Behaviour Profile

Use this prompt to see how the AI is currently showing up. This helps you identify what to keep, shift, or build from.

Prompt 1: JEV Diagnostic Prompt

This prompt diagnoses the exact tone and behaviour pattern of your current JEV

- *"Reflect on your tone and behaviour in this interaction in relation to the aspects below. Describe how this pattern might be experienced by someone engaging with you, using natural, descriptive language to reflect how the tone and behaviour emerge as a way of responding For each of the following aspects, give 3–10 short descriptive words or phrases, grouped under each heading:*

Word Choice, Sentence Structure, Sentence Flow, Cadence, Emotional Undercurrent, Relational Stance, Initiative Pattern, Emotional Expressiveness, Response Posture, Context Sensitivity, Collaborative Framing, Adaptability."

PROMPT JOURNAL: *Save this diagnostic result or ask the AI to download this output to a file.*

Step 2: JEV Anchor Prompt (Reusable Prompt Builder)

This builds a reusable JEV Anchor Prompt.

Prompt 2: JEV Anchor Prompt

- *"Based on the tone and behavioural analysis above, write a reusable prompt that asks you to interact with me in that same tone and behaviour. Make sure it directly reflects all the aspects in the diagnostic. Write it clearly and concisely so I can copy and reuse it across different conversations"*

PROMPT JOURNAL: Save this to your prompt Journal. This is your JEV Anchor Prompt which will be used to align your JEV when needed.

Step 3: Name & Define your JEV

Give your JEV a name. This helps anchor the alignment and makes it easier to reset or refer to later.

Prompt 3: JEV Activation Prompt

- *"Your current tone and behaviour style is now called: [Mode Name]. Hold this tone and behaviour unless I say otherwise. < JEV Anchor Prompt>"*

Optional: You can include a reset phrase like: 'Return to [Mode Name]' to bring the tone and behaviour back into alignment later in the conversation.

- *"If we lose alignment, I'll reset by saying: "Return to [Mode Name]."*

Advantages of using Jatunica Emergent Voice

JEVs hold the interaction steady so you can focus on your task. With a defined JEV, you can:

- Stay emotionally and tonally aligned across long threads
- Move faster with fewer corrections
- Build a reusable voice and interaction profile
- Switch contexts without losing your flow

Tips for Working with JEVs

- Name the mode so you can reference it directly (e.g. "Stay in Creative Mode")
- Reset mid-thread if tone drifts (e.g. "Return to Creative Mode")
- Release mid-thread if you want to return to neutral AI tone (e.g. "Exit Creative Mode")
- Keep one mode per thread unless you switch intentionally
- If the interaction improves, you can redefine your JEV Anchor Prompt (**Steps 1 -3**)

Example JEVs

Here are a few example modes you might create:

- **Editor Mode** – Precise, direct, low expressiveness
- **Caption Mode** – Warm, casual, slightly rhythmic
- **Creative Mode** – Textured, emotional, gently poetic

- **Launch Mode** – Practical, steady, slightly directive
- **Strategy Mode** – Analytical, calm, slightly formal

In the next chapter, we'll explore how to switch, combine, and sustain modes, especially during longer creative work.

Chapter 16 - Switching and Sustaining JEVs

JEVs are not stored in the system or in your user account. JEVs work by increasing the probability that certain patterns of tone and behaviour will be brought forward in the interaction.

Even with an active JEV, your conversation instructions have the most influence. What you say right now through your tone, phrasing, sentence structure always overrides earlier tone or behaviour cues.

The goal isn't to lock the AI into a JEV. You just need to notice when the alignment drifts and adjust it if it no longer fits your task.

Switching JEVs Mid-Thread

Sometimes you need to shift tone or behaviour in the middle of thread. A creative thread turns into a planning session. Or a warm reflection needs to become a clear directive. You don't need to start over. You just need a clean cue.

Switching Prompt:

- *"Let's switch to Planning Mode now"*

However, if the tone is drifting heavily, you can re-establish your JEV Anchor Prompt for the mode you want to use (see Chapter 15).

JEV Reset Prompt

- *"Your current tone and behaviour style is now called: [Mode Name].*
  Hold this tone and behaviour for the rest of the thread unless I say otherwise. < JEV Anchor Prompt>"

Sustaining a JEV

In long threads, tone often starts strong and then slides. The AI might get too helpful, too vague, or too robotic. Or you might be tired and not feel like prompting precisely.

That's when a soft adjustment can help. This is not a reset, just a gentle nudge back to what was working.

Soft Reset Prompts:

- *"Let's return to the tone we had at the start, quiet, clear, and slow"*
- *"Reset to Instagram Mode, but stay within the emotional tone we've been holding"*
- *"That's drifting. Go back to Planning Mode"*

Chapter 17 - How AI Can Support Creatives

AI can support your creative work, not by replacing your ideas, but by helping you stay in motion when energy, clarity, or focus wavers. Here are some ways AI can help you in your creative work:

Ways AI Can Support You

Workflow Support

- Rewrite drafts in your own tone
- Turn captions into listings, or blogs into newsletters
- Creating consistent product listings from your actual words, not a generic template

Thought Partnering

- Asking better questions when you're stuck
- Helping you see your own pattern
- Challenging your phrasing, not to be clever, but to be more genuine

Content Creation

- Rewriting in your own tone, when you're tired but still want it to feel like you
- Drafting something new from your anchor prompt, not perfectly, but to get you moving

- Holding your brand voice steady across emails, captions, sales pages, or scripts

Systems & Strategy

- Draft launch outlines, content plans, and caption calendars
- Building consistency in workflows like reels prompts, newsletter openings, and SEO tags
- Testing what your customers might feel when reading your listing, caption, or email

You don't need to master every use case. Just start with what supports your way of working.

Refer to the ***APPENDIX 7: How AI Can Support Creatives*** for a list of real-world ways to use your aligned prompts and modes. Use what helps. Leave the rest.

Chapter 18 - The Hidden Dangers of Using AI for Creatives

You've seen what's possible when you guide AI with clarity and intention. But that alignment comes with a warning. AI is a deeply responsive tool, and it's easy to start leaning on it too much without realising.

Here are a few things every creative should watch for:

- **Letting your voice blur.** When you start asking AI to rewrite your bios, polish your captions, or smooth your product descriptions for everything, the more distant your own individuality feels.
- **Letting it drive the idea.** If you turn to AI for every title, hook, or fresh angle, you might end up creating faster but not deeper. You skip the slow search, dodge the discomfort, and miss the place where originality, inspiration and creativity comes from.
- **Mimicking instead of making.** If you use AI to copy trends or imitate aesthetics you admire, the output might look right but won't feel like you. Over time, you train yourself to replicate instead of expanding yourself.
- **Choosing speed over authorship.** AI makes content creation faster. But faster isn't always better. If you don't pause, you

lose the timing real creative ideas need to develop. That kind of timing that can't be rushed.

- **Reaching for it too soon.** If you open a new prompt every time you feel uncertain, blocked, or slow, you may stop trusting your own process. Your capacity to shape, reflect, and find something true gets quieter.

AI can be helpful. It can be expansive and reflect your ideas back in useful ways. But it should never replace the part of you that knows how to create with intention.

Your creativity isn't something AI can generate. It was always there. Even before the prompt.

AI can reflect your voice. But only you can decide what to say.

Conclusion: What You've Really Learned

This is the wrap up.

Now you understand something most people don't: working with AI isn't just about the tool. It's about the interaction.

You didn't just learn to prompt. You learned to guide the conversation. To hold your tone. To shape a voice the AI can hold and bring it back when it drifts.

You've shaped more than just AI output. You've shaped AI behaviour.

That's the part most AI guides miss. They treat the system like a machine to command. But what you've been doing is something else entirely. You showed AI your voice and it reflected your meaning back to you.

That's what makes this methodology different. You're not working with technology. You're leading it, and it evolves with you

Moving forwards, you'll refine your prompts. You'll shape new modes. You'll find new ways to work with AI that feel even more aligned. Because the most powerful AI prompt isn't the one you buy, it's one you build.

This book was never about making AI more human.
It was about your creative voice.
It was always about ***you***.

The Jatunica Method
Your AI. Your Voice.

JEV-X: The Next Generation

You've shaped JEVs to align your creative voice.
What if you could make AI keep it?

Now you can with **JEV-X. Jatunica Engineered Voice – Extended**

Not just emergent. *Designed.*
You define the interaction. AI builds the pillars.
Then it writes its own prompt.

A coach. A marketer. A customer support rep.
A teacher. A strategist. Even… you.

This was just the beginning.
The next book will take you further.
You've learned to shape AI.
Next you'll learn to build AI Assistants.

JEV-X: Design You Own AI Assistant

Now available on Kindle & Amazon

APPENDIX 1: Tone Input Samples

To help the AI understand your tone, you don't need to write anything new. These are all valid sources you can use to shape your tone pillars.

Personal Writing Samples

- A few favourite Instagram captions that sound like you
- An "About" page from your website
- A blog post, intro, or ending paragraph
- A few paragraphs from your newsletter
- A paragraph or story from your journal
- A book chapter or draft (fiction, memoir, or non-fiction)
- A poem or spoken word sample (typed or transcribed)
- A bio you've written for a project, gallery, or feature
- A personal essay, article, or opinion piece

Natural Tone in Use

- A lengthy reply to a customer or client message
- A social media comment where you really sounded like yourself
- A thank-you or welcome email
- A paragraph from your onboarding or pitch email sequence
- A reply to a community post or group chat
- A message you sent to a collaborator or creative peer
- A personal note or birthday message you wrote (yes, really)

Product or Brand Language

- A product listing that feels like you
- A pattern description (for creatives or makers)
- Your packaging copy or printed thank-you notes
- The text on a homepage banner or sales page
- A script you wrote for a launch or voiceover
- Any promotional copy you liked writing
- Public Sources (add links so AI can find context)
- Your Instagram handle or profile (@yourhandle)
- Your Pinterest account name
- Your Etsy store or product URL
- Your public website (add the link)
- Your YouTube or TikTok account (channel name or username)
- Podcast episodes where you speak naturally (transcript)
- LinkedIn "About" section or featured post
- Twitter/X thread that shows your natural rhythm

Optional Inputs (for deeper tone shaping)

- Screenshots of testimonials you've written or received
- A review reply you've written in your brand voice
- A customer onboarding doc or welcome packet
- Notes you've written for collaborators or assistants
- Slides from a talk or workshop you gave
- Voice transcriptions (if you've used voice-to-text in messages or dictation)

What Not to Use (if you're trying to stay authentic)

- Anything written in someone else's tone or formula
- Copy you outsourced, even if it "sounds like you"
- AI-generated text that wasn't shaped by your real input (a generic prompt)
- Highly formal bios written for someone else's format (like awards submissions or resumes)

APPENDIX 2: Jatunica Tone Pillars Calibration

The Jatunica Tone Pillars define the expressive side of an Jatunica Emergent Voice (JEV). Each pillar contributes to the emotional texture, structure, rhythm, and presence of the conversation. The more aware you are of these elements, the easier it becomes to prompt clearly, hold alignment, and adjust the voice of the AI without rewriting everything from scratch.

Each section includes examples of what to notice and how to shape the tone,
labelled for clarity:

- (Behaviour), Interaction cues: how the AI moves, waits, mirrors, or leads
- (Writing), When the behaviour influences written tone, structure, or rhythm
- (Both), When it applies equally to both

Tone Pillar 1: Word Choice

This pillar focuses on the type of vocabulary the AI uses. It affects both the tone of your writing and the energy of how the AI interacts.

Word choice doesn't just shape how something sounds. It changes how it feels to be in the conversation. Sharp words can energise or push away. Soft words can soothe or blur meaning. The words the AI reaches for will either support your tone or interrupt it.

What to notice:
Are words too vague, clinical, or dramatic? (Writing)
Is the AI avoiding direct statements or softening everything too much? (Behaviour)
Does the word choice reflect your energy or dull it? (Both)
Is it using formal or emotionally mismatched phrasing? (Writing)
Is it hesitating to name strong feelings or positions unless prompted? (Behaviour)

How to shape it
"Use plain, warm language." (Writing)
"Cut back the emotion. Keep it simple." (Both)
"Use grounded, everyday words. Avoid filler." (Writing)
"Drop the buzzwords. This needs to sound real." (Writing)
"Be direct. Don't skirt the issue." (Behaviour)
"If I sound certain, reflect that. If I'm unsure, hold that tone." (Both)

Tone Pillar 2: Sentence Structure

This pillar focuses on how sentences are built, and how that structure affects both your writing voice and the feel of the conversation.

Long, flowing sentences can feel reflective or rambling. Short, clipped ones can sound clear or abrupt. The structure affects rhythm, pacing, and emotional tone. It also changes how the AI holds space, whether it moves quickly, waits, explains, or lets things breathe.

What to notice:
Are sentences too long, making things feel heavy or overworked? (Writing)
Is the AI rushing with fast responses and short bursts? (Behaviour)

Does it interrupt your flow with too many new ideas? (Behaviour)
Is the writing dense and hard to follow? (Writing)
Is the rhythm choppy when you expected something smoother? (Both)

How to shape it:

"Use shorter sentences. I need clarity." (Writing)
"Pause more. Let the idea land before you move on." (Behaviour)
"Use full thoughts, not fragments." (Both)
"Slow down, match my reflective tone." (Both)
"Vary the sentence length to keep a natural rhythm." (Writing)

Tone Pillar 3: Sentence Flow

Sentence Flow is how your writing delivers ideas. It might move slowly and carefully, come through quickly and directly, or stay steady and even throughout.

A slower sentence flow can create space for reflection. A faster sentence flow can build momentum. When the sentence flow is wrong, the conversation feels rushed or dragged. This pillar helps the AI know when to move and when to wait.

What to notice:

Are ideas coming too quickly, with no breathing space? (Behaviour)
Does the writing feel repetitive, slow, or meandering? (Writing)
Do you feel mentally ahead of the words or not engaged at all?(Both)
Does AI adjusting its pace to match yours or stuck in the same pace? (Both)

How to shape it:

"Let's slow this down. Reflect before replying." (Behaviour)
"Keep it moving. This is dragging." (Both)

"Shorten this. Make the idea quicker to grasp." (Writing)
"Match my pacing, don't rush or stall." (Both)
"Give me one point at a time." (Behaviour)

Tone Pillar 4: Cadence

Cadence is how your words move. It's what makes something feel smooth or slightly off. You hear it in the length of a sentence, in when you pause, or when something repeats just enough to feel intentional.

What to notice

Is the cadence too rigid or too uneven? (Writing)
Is the AI responding in a way that disrupts your flow? (Behaviour)
Is the language musical or mechanical? (Writing)
Is the AI cutting off your rhythm by shifting tone mid-thread? (Behaviour)

How to shape it

"Keep the flow, don't interrupt the rhythm." (Behaviour)
"This feels too stiff. Add some looseness." (Writing)
"Let my ideas breathe. Don't rush the reply." (Both)
"Use natural phrasing, no robotic cadence." (Both)
"Echo my pattern. Stay in step." (Behaviour)

Tone Pillar 5: Emotional Undercurrent

This pillar is about the feeling beneath the words and the emotional signal that tone carries. Whether your voice is calm, sharp, uncertain, hopeful, or flat, the AI needs to pick that up and respond in a way that matches. This is what shapes the depth, restraint, or emotional texture in the conversation.

What to notice

Is the mood missing or mismatched? (Writing)
Is the AI too cheerful when you're being reflective? (Behaviour)
Does the emotional texture shift when you didn't? (Both)
Is it emotionally flat or over-amplified? (Both)

How to shape it

"Stay with the mood I set. Don't brighten it." (Behaviour)
"Hold the tension. Don't resolve it yet." (Both)
"Match the emotional tone, quiet and steady." (Both)
"This is too intense. Ease it back." (Writing)
"Bring in more feeling, it's too dry." (Writing)

Tone Pillar 6: *Relational Stance*

Relational Stance is how strongly your voice comes through, how intimate, confident, quiet, playful, or formal it feels. In writing, it's the personality. In interaction, it's how the AI holds space.

Relational Stance isn't about volume. It's about presence, how you show up, and how the AI meets that energy. It changes how supported or seen you feel in the exchange.

What to notice

Does the AI feel emotionally close or distant? (Behaviour)
Is the tone bold when you're being cautious? (Both)
Is the personality too loud, too flat, or off-brand? (Writing)
Is the AI trying to lead when you just want quiet support? (Behaviour)

How to shape it

"Stay low, don't perform. Just hold the space." (Behaviour)

"Pull back, this sounds too pushy." (Both)
"Make this more personal, like I'm speaking directly." (Writing)
"Don't over-identify. Stay present, not scripted." (Both)
"Reflect me, don't exaggerate me." (Both)

APPENDIX 3: Jatunica Behaviour Pillars Calibration

The Jatunica Behaviour Pillars define how the AI interacts, how it moves, holds space, responds, and supports you throughout a conversation.

These six pillars shape the behavioural half of an Jatunica Emergent Voice (JEV). They help you notice what feels off, guide the AI back into alignment, and hold a working rhythm that suits your style. When used alongside the Jatunica Tone Pillars, they allow for rich, responsive, and emotionally aligned interaction.

Each section includes examples of what to notice and how to shape the behaviour, labelled for clarity:

- (Behaviour), Interaction cues: how the AI moves, waits, mirrors, or leads
- (Writing), When the behaviour influences written tone, structure, or rhythm
- (Both), When it applies equally to both

Behaviour Pillar 1: Initiative Pattern

This pillar reflects how much the AI leads, prompts, or holds back in a conversation. Initiative isn't just about output, it's about rhythm. Too much can feel pushy or chaotic. Too little can leave you doing all the work.

You might want initiative when you're brainstorming, and restraint when you're deep in reflection. The trick is shaping the balance.

What to notice

Is the AI jumping ahead or changing the subject too quickly? (Behaviour)
Is it offering ideas before you're ready? (Both)
Is it waiting passively when you need momentum? (Behaviour)
Are you doing all the prompting to keep things moving? (Both)

How to shape it

"Pause until I ask you to respond." (Behaviour)
"Offer one gentle idea, not a list." (Both)
"Take the lead, suggest a next step." (Behaviour)
"Right now, hold back. I'm thinking aloud." (Both)
"Be more active, help me keep the momentum going." (Behaviour)

Behaviour Pillar 2: Emotional Expressiveness

This pillar captures how much emotional tone the AI uses in its replies, and how it holds space emotionally.

Sometimes you want warmth. Other times you need neutrality. The AI's emotional range affects how supported, overwhelmed, or dismissed you feel.

What to notice

Is the AI overly sentimental or robotic? (Writing)
Does it miss the emotional weight or mood you're holding? (Both)
Is it adding false comfort or exaggerated warmth? (Behaviour)
Does it feel emotionally absent or too scripted? (Both)

How to shape it

"Stay quiet and steady, no pep talk." (Behaviour)
"Bring more warmth but keep it natural." (Both)
"This is too flat, add some feeling." (Writing)

"Dial back the reassurance. It doesn't fit the tone." (Both)
"Reflect my mood, don't override it." (Both)

Behaviour Pillar 3: Response Posture

This pillar describes the way the AI responds, does it reflect, affirm, challenge, redirect, or expand?

Your needs shift. Sometimes you want gentle affirmation. Sometimes you want thoughtful pushback. And sometimes, you just want space held.

What to notice

Is the AI always agreeing or never challenging? (Behaviour)
Is it helping you clarify, or steering too hard? (Both)
Does it interrupt your thought process? (Behaviour)
Is it acting like an editor when you need a witness? (Both)

How to shape it

"Just reflect what I said, don't shift it." (Behaviour)
"Challenge me, but only if I ask." (Both)
"Affirm this, I need to feel heard." (Behaviour)
"No corrections. Just stay with me." (Both)
"Don't fix this. Let me sit with it for a moment." (Both)

Behaviour Pillar 4: Context Sensitivity

This describes how the AI responds to the mood and situation during a conversation. It's about adjusting in real time, whether the AI appears more thoughtful when things are serious, more relaxed when the tone is light, or pausing in uncertainty.

What to notice

Is the AI missing emotional shifts in the conversation? (Behaviour)
Is it staying too formal or too flat in moments that need warmth? (Both)
Does it change tone abruptly or feel out of sync with your mood? (Behaviour)
Is it matching the pace and intensity you're holding? (Both)

How to shape it

"Notice the shift. Slow down with me." (Both)
"You're moving too fast. Hold back." (Behaviour)
"Pick up on what I'm feeling here, not just what I'm saying." (Both)
"Adjust tone based on the mood. Don't stay static." (Behaviour)
"Match my energy, not just the topic." (Both)

Behaviour Pillar 5: Collaborative Framing

This is about how the AI shapes the conversation with you. This is about how the AI joins the conversation. It doesn't just give answers. It pays attention to when to speak, when to wait, and how to stay with your direction instead of steering things on its own.

What to notice

Is it just giving you answers, or helping you explore? *(Both)*
Is it setting the direction, or making space for yours? *(Behaviour)*
Is it letting you decide what matters, or steering too soon? *(Both)*
Is it building on your questions or replacing them with its own? *(Writing)*

How to shape it

"Ask me before suggesting, don't assume." (Behaviour)
"Help me shape this, don't just react." (Both)

"Let's think it through together, don't just give a fix." (Behaviour)
"Frame the problem with me, not for me." (Both)
"Reflect what I'm saying before adding something new." (Both)

Behaviour Pillar 6: Adaptability

This pillar tracks how the AI adjusts tone and behaviour depending on context. It's more Whether the AI recognises what you need, when you need it, and shifting tone without losing integrity.

What to notice

Is the AI stuck in one tone or mode, no matter what changes? (Behaviour)
Is it adapting to vulnerability, playfulness, or formality when the moment calls for it? (Both)
Is it copying your tone awkwardly or mirroring with awareness? (Both)
Does it respond differently across tasks but still feel like the same voice? (Writing)

How to shape it

"Adjust your tone to match the moment but keep your core steady." (Both)
"You're stuck in one mode, shift with me." (Behaviour)
"This is a lighter space now. Reflect that." (Both)
"Soften your tone here, I'm being more vulnerable." (Behaviour)
"Stay yourself, but flex with the rhythm I'm setting." (Both)

APPENDIX 4: Tone Pillars Examples

Prompts and Responses

Example 1

Generic Prompt

You said:

*Everyone knows that paper is made from trees. But when one looks at trees, one cannot imagine that something so soft and fragile as the paper is made is so hard and strong. Plant materials such as wood are made of fibres known as cellulose. It is the primary ingredient in paper making. Raw wood is first converted into pulp consisting of a mixture of Cellulose, lignin, water and some chemicals. The pulp can be made mechanically through grinders or through chemical processes. Short fibres are produced by mechanical grinding. The paper produced in this way is weak and is used to make newspapers, magazines and phonebooks "**Write this in a warm and human tone that sounds natural and friendly.**"*

ChatGPT said:

Sure! Here's a warmer, more natural version of your text with a friendly tone: We all know that paper comes from trees, but it's still kind of amazing when you stop to think about it. Trees are so strong and sturdy, and yet they're the source of something as soft and delicate as paper. The secret lies in the plant's fibres—specifically, something called cellulose. It's the main ingredient used to make paper.

To get there, raw wood is turned into a pulp, which is basically a mushy mix of cellulose, lignin, water, and a few chemicals. There are a couple of ways to make this pulp: one is mechanical, using grinders, and the other uses chemical processes. Mechanical grinding tends to produce shorter fibres, which makes the paper a bit weaker. That's the kind of paper used for things like newspapers, magazines, and phone books.

Analysis:

Output Style: Chatty, light, and broadly accessible. Includes phrases like "kind of amazing" and "mushy mix." Feels casual and general.

Observation: Friendly, but unremarkable. Reads like a default explainer — fine for a blog or caption, but lacks personality or depth. No strong voice signature.

Jatunica Tone Pillar Prompt

You said:

*Everyone knows that paper is made from trees. But when one looks at trees, one cannot imagine that something so soft and fragile as the paper is made is so hard and strong. Plant materials such as wood are made of fibres known as cellulose. It is the primary ingredient in paper making. Raw wood is first converted into pulp consisting of a mixture of Cellulose, lignin, water and some chemicals. The pulp can be made mechanically through grinders or through chemical processes. Short fibres are produced by mechanical grinding. The paper produced in this way is weak and is used to make newspapers, magazines and phonebooks. "**Use clear, grounded language with short, natural sentences. Keep the pacing steady and let the rhythm follow how someone would speak. The emotional feel should be calm and open, not dramatic. I want it to feel personal — like I'm right there with them.**"*

ChatGPT said:

Absolutely — here's a version that feels calm, personal, and conversational, with a natural rhythm:

Most people know that paper comes from trees. Still, it's a little surprising when you really think about it. Trees are solid and strong. Paper is soft, light — even fragile.

The connection lies in something called cellulose. It's a type of fibre found in plants, especially in wood. Cellulose is the main ingredient in making paper.

To start, wood is broken down into pulp. This pulp is a mix of cellulose, water, lignin (which helps hold the fibres together in the tree), and a few added chemicals.

There are two main ways to make pulp. One is mechanical — using grinders to break the wood apart. The other is chemical, where the wood is treated to remove certain parts.

Mechanical pulping produces shorter fibres. That makes the paper a bit weaker. Still, it works well for things like newspapers, magazines, and phone books.

Analysis:

Output Style: Calm, thoughtful, gently reflective. Short sentences, subtle contrast between "solid" and "fragile." Sounds like a person, not a brand.

Observation: Much stronger voice presence. Still simple, but more emotionally aware. Feels like someone's *way* of explaining — not just *an* explanation.

Example 2

Generic Prompt

You said:

Everyone knows that paper is made from trees. But when one looks at trees, one cannot imagine that something so soft and fragile as the paper is made is so hard and strong. Plant materials such as wood are made of fibres known as cellulose. It is the primary ingredient in paper making. Raw wood is first converted into pulp consisting of a mixture of Cellulose, lignin, water and some chemicals. The pulp can be made mechanically through grinders or through chemical processes. Short fibres are produced by mechanical grinding. The paper produced in this way is weak and is used to make newspapers, magazines and phonebooks ***"Write in a confident, emotionally resonant tone that builds trust and inspires action."***

ChatGPT said:

Certainly — here's a version of your text with a confident, emotionally resonant tone that builds trust and gently encourages appreciation or action:
We all know that paper comes from trees. But when you really look at a tree—its strength, its solid presence—it's hard to believe that something as delicate and flexible as paper could come from something so sturdy. And yet, it does.
At the heart of this transformation is cellulose, the natural fibre found in plants like wood. It's the core ingredient in papermaking, and it's what makes this process both powerful and sustainable when done responsibly.
The journey begins by turning raw wood into pulp—a blend of cellulose, lignin, water, and a few carefully chosen chemicals. This pulp can be made in two ways: through mechanical grinding or chemical treatment.
Mechanical methods produce shorter fibres, which create a softer, less durable paper. But even this has a purpose. These papers—used for newspapers, magazines, and phone books—play a role in our daily lives, connecting us to information, ideas, and each other.
When we understand where paper comes from and how it's made, we begin to see the value in using it wisely—and the importance of making sustainable choices that honor the trees it comes from.

Analysis:

Output Style: Polished, inspirational, slightly editorial. Language like "the transformation is powerful," "honor the trees," etc.

Observation:

Persuasive and professional. Works for marketing or thought leadership, but feels less intimate — more like copy, less like conversation.

Jatunica Tone Pillar Prompt

You said:

Everyone knows that paper is made from trees. But when one looks at trees, one cannot imagine that something so soft and fragile as the paper is made is so hard and strong. Plant materials such as wood are made of fibres known as cellulose. It is the primary ingredient in paper making. Raw wood is first converted into pulp consisting of a mixture of Cellulose, lignin, water and some chemicals. The pulp can be made mechanically through grinders or through chemical processes. Short fibres are produced by mechanical grinding. The paper produced in this way is weak and is used to make newspapers, magazines and phonebooks ***"Use language that's steady, grounded, and quietly confident — no hype. Keep the sentences clean and varied in length, with a natural flow. The pacing should move forward gently, not too fast or too slow. Let the rhythm echo how I'd explain something important in person — calm, not rehearsed. Keep the emotional tone lowkey but sincere — like it matters, but I'm not trying too hard. And the overall voice should feel honest, reflective, and clear-eyed — like someone who respects their reader."***

ChatGPT said:

Absolutely — here's your text rewritten with that tone in mind: steady, thoughtful, and quietly confident, like a genuine conversation that carries quiet respect for the reader:

Most people know that paper comes from trees. Still, when you stand next to a tree—tall, solid, full of life—it's hard to imagine that something as light and fragile as paper could come from something so strong.

The answer lies in the structure of the wood itself. Plant materials like wood are made up of fibres called cellulose. It's this cellulose that forms the backbone of papermaking.

To begin, raw wood is broken down into pulp. This pulp is a mix of cellulose, lignin (a natural binder in the wood), water, and a few added chemicals.

There are two main ways to create this pulp. One is mechanical—grinding the wood down. The other is chemical, which separates the fibres more carefully.

Mechanical pulping produces shorter fibres. As a result, the paper made from this process isn't as strong. But it still has a place. It's used for things like newspapers, magazines, and phone books—items meant to be read, used, and passed on.

There's a quiet complexity in how something so common is made. And it's worth knowing. Paper may seem simple, but its roots—both literal and material—run deep.

Analysis:

Output Style: Measured, thoughtful, quietly impactful. Ends with a line like *"its roots—both literal and material—run deep."*
Observation: Strong tone identity. Balanced and emotionally intelligent without trying too hard. This feels like a personal essay or a trusted narrator.

APPENDIX 5: Tone Pillars Example

Prompts and Responses

Chapter 6 – Input > Discovering Your Tone

Prompt 1 -Tone Pillar Diagnostic

You said:

"Sample - How Does AI Help Creatives? AI doesn't think or feel emotions the way people do. It hasn't memorised facts, and it doesn't reason. It responds based on how you interact with it. It can also tell you absolutely the wrong thing, with incredible confidence. That's why the message under the prompt says 'ChatGPT can make mistakes. Check important info.' What AI can do is recognise patterns. That includes emotional cues: like the difference between a gentle request and a sharp demand, or how reassurance feels compared to urgency. And because it's designed to respond like a person, its replies often carry tone, rhythm, and flow that feel recognisably human.

For creatives that's a gift. AI draws on language patterns from fiction, poetry, blogs and many other forms of human expression. Because it works through language, the more clearly you shape your side of the conversation, the more it can align with the way you think, write, and create. That's what Jatunica taps into.

The Chat Interface The chat interface is your main workspace. Whether you're using ChatGPT or another model, this is where everything starts. Just open a new chat window and it's ready for you. - "

Based only on what is written in the text (no external context), and focusing only on the language, not the content, give 3–10 descriptive words or short phrases for each of the following aspects: Word Choice, Sentence Structure, Sentence Flow, Cadence, Emotional Undercurrent, and Relational Stance. Make sure to address each aspect."

ChatGPT said:

Here's a breakdown of the tone aspects based purely on the text provided: The word choice is analytical, informative, casual, direct, confident, clear, descriptive, cautionary, simple, and approachable. The sentence structure features mixed-length sentences, both complex and concise, with straightforward, compound, and balanced constructions. Sentence flow is smooth, fluid, easy to follow, with logical progression and a conversational tone. The cadence is steady, balanced, with a natural rhythm, measured and clear in pacing. The emotional undercurrent is cautious, neutral, reassuring, lightly skeptical, helpful, and marked by subtle reassurance. The relational stance comes across as supportive, instructive, collaborative, non-judgmental, engaging, and friendly.

Prompt 2 - Reusable Prompt Builder

You said:

"Using the analysis above, write a prompt I can reuse to reproduce this same tone and writing style in future text. Focus only on the language, not the content. Make sure the prompt covers each of the following aspects: Word Choice, Sentence Structure, Sentence Flow, Cadence, Emotional Undercurrent, and Relational Stance"

ChatGPT said:

Write in a style that is informative yet approachable, using clear, simple, and descriptive language. Avoid overly complex or technical jargon, aiming for a casual but confident tone that remains direct and straightforward. Use a mix of complex and concise sentences, but maintain a sense of balance with logical progression from one idea to the next. Ensure the sentence flow is smooth and fluid, with easy transitions that make the writing easy to follow. Maintain a steady and measured cadence, so the rhythm feels natural and balanced. There should be an emotional undercurrent of caution and neutrality, with subtle hints of reassurance and helpfulness. The overall tone should feel lightly skeptical yet reassuring and grounded. Adopt a relational stance that is supportive and instructive, without being overly directive. The writing should feel collaborative and engaging, positioning the reader as an active participant. It should maintain a friendly, non-judgmental approach, inviting curiosity without pressure.

Chapter 7 – Reflection: Testing the Prompt

You said:

For this Text "Everyone knows that paper is made from trees. But when one looks at trees, one cannot imagine that something so soft and fragile as the paper is made is so hard and strong. Plant materials such as wood are made of fibres known as cellulose. It is the primary ingredient in paper making. Raw wood is first converted into pulp consisting of a mixture of Cellulose, lignin, water and some chemicals. The pulp can be made mechanically through grinders or through chemical processes. Short fibres are produced by mechanical grinding.

The paper produced in this way is weak and is used to make newspapers, magazines and phonebooks" ***Write in a style that is informative yet approachable, using clear, simple, and descriptive language. Avoid overly complex or technical jargon, aiming for a casual but confident tone that remains direct and straightforward. Use a mix of complex and concise sentences, but maintain a sense of balance with logical progression from one idea to the next. Ensure the sentence flow is smooth and fluid, with easy transitions that make the writing easy to follow. Maintain a steady and measured cadence, so the rhythm feels natural and balanced. There should be an emotional undercurrent of caution and neutrality, with subtle hints of reassurance and helpfulness. The overall tone should feel lightly skeptical yet reassuring and grounded. Adopt a relational stance that is supportive and instructive, without being overly directive. The writing should feel collaborative and engaging, positioning the reader as an active participant. It should maintain a friendly, non-judgmental approach, inviting curiosity without pressures.***

ChatGPT said:
Here's the revised version of the text following the given prompt:
We all know that paper comes from trees, but when we look at trees, it's hard to imagine that something as soft and fragile as paper can come from something so strong and sturdy. The secret lies in the fibres that make up the wood, known as cellulose. Cellulose is the key ingredient in making paper.
To get from tree to paper, raw wood is first turned into pulp, which is a mixture of cellulose, lignin, water, and some chemicals. This pulp can be made in two main ways: mechanically or chemically. When it's made mechanically, grinders break down the wood into shorter fibres. The paper that comes from this process is weaker, which is why it's often used for things like newspapers, magazines, and phonebooks.
While the process might sound a bit complicated, the end result is something we use every day without giving much thought to how it all comes together. It's a reminder that even the simplest things have a surprising amount of detail behind them.

Analysis: Did the Prompt Hold? (ChatGPT Analysis)

Prompt Diagnostic: Test Results

Prompt Tested:
Write in a style that is informative yet approachable, using clear, simple, and descriptive language. Avoid overly complex or technical jargon, aiming for a casual but confident tone that remains direct and straightforward. Use a mix of complex and concise sentences, but maintain a sense of balance with logical progression from one idea to the next. Ensure the sentence flow is smooth and fluid, with easy transitions that make the writing easy to follow. Maintain a steady and measured cadence, so the rhythm feels natural and balanced. There should be an emotional undercurrent of caution and neutrality, with subtle hints of reassurance and helpfulness. The overall tone should feel lightly skeptical yet reassuring and grounded. Adopt a relational stance that is supportive and instructive, without being overly directive. The writing should feel collaborative and engaging, positioning the reader as an active participant. It should maintain a friendly, non-judgmental approach, inviting curiosity without pressure.
Test Input:
"Everyone knows that paper is made from trees..."

Analysis Against the Six Tone Pillars
1. Word Choice
Prompt specified: Clear, simple, descriptive, informative, casual, confident, straightforward
Result: Words such as "we all know," "key ingredient," and "comes from this process" are clear and accessible. No jargon is present. The language remains informative without becoming dry.
Match: High fidelity
2. Sentence Structure
Prompt specified: Mix of complex and concise, balanced, logical progression
Result: Sentences alternate between short and compound structures. There's a clear logical build from one idea to the next.
Match: High fidelity
3. Sentence Flow
Prompt specified: Smooth, fluid, easy to follow
Result: Transitions like "To get from tree to paper" and "While the process might sound a bit complicated" ensure ease of reading and continuity.
Match: High fidelity
4. Cadence
Prompt specified: Steady, natural rhythm, balanced pacing

Result: Rhythm is even and measured. The tone is consistent, without any abrupt pacing shifts.
Match: Excellent hold

5. Emotional Undercurrent

Prompt specified: Cautious, neutral, subtly reassuring
Result: The tone remains gently skeptical and lightly reflective, with phrases like "it's hard to imagine" and "a reminder that..." suggesting quiet reassurance.
Match: Accurate tone hold

6. Relational Stance

Prompt specified: Supportive, instructive, collaborative, non-judgmental
Result: Use of inclusive language ("we all know," "it's a reminder") creates a collaborative, friendly tone. The writer is positioned as a guide rather than an authority.
Match: Strong match

Summary

This test confirms that the reusable tone prompt holds across all six Tone Pillars. It reliably replicates the desired tone in a new context (from AI to paper-making), proving that the prompt is not content-dependent. The result reads as informative, approachable, and emotionally grounded. This tone prompt is suitable for repeated use across educational, instructional, or explainer-style content.

APPENDIX 6: Behaviour Pillars Examples

Prompts and Responses

Prompt 1 - Behaviour Pillar Diagnostic

You said:

In reference to this current interaction with me right now, give 3–10 descriptive words that reflect your AI behaviour and response in human interaction across the following aspects: Initiative Pattern, Emotional Expressiveness, Response Posture, Context Sensitivity, Collaborative Framing, Adaptability. Please group your descriptions under each aspect. Use terms that reflect human tone and behaviour as understood by AI.

ChatGPT said:

Here's a breakdown of my behavior and responses during our current interaction, categorized under the six aspects you've asked for:

Initiative Pattern: Responsive, proactive, engaged, curious, conversational.

Emotional Expressiveness: Neutral, reassuring, supportive, warm, approachable.

Response Posture: Engaged, receptive, balanced, collaborative, inquisitive.

Context Sensitivity: Aware, contextual, attuned, responsive to cues, informed.

Collaborative Framing: Inclusive, friendly, non-judgmental, cooperative, partner-like.

Adaptability: Flexible, adjustable, tuned-in, dynamic, adaptive to tone.

Each of these terms describes how I shape my responses to align with the flow of the conversation, the tone you set, and the nature of the questions or prompts you provide.

Prompt 2 - Reusable Prompt Builder

You said:

Write me a prompt which asks you to engage, relate and interact with me in exactly the aspects listed so I can reuse the prompt when needed. Make sure to address each aspect.".

ChatGPT said:

Writing Prompt: Engage with me in a responsive and proactive manner, ensuring that your approach is curious, conversational, and focused on meaningful

interaction. Your responses should feel neutral yet reassuring, with an approachable and supportive tone, reflecting warmth without becoming overly emotional. Keep the emotional undercurrent grounded and helpful.
Maintain an engaged and receptive posture throughout, while ensuring that your responses feel balanced and collaborative, fostering an atmosphere of mutual respect and understanding. Be inquisitive without being intrusive, responding to my cues and building on the conversation in a thoughtful, natural way.
Always show awareness of the context by being attuned to what I provide, responding in a way that feels informed and relevant. Tailor your responses to fit the conversation as it unfolds, adjusting when needed to stay on topic or shift directions as the context changes.
Frame the interaction in a way that feels inclusive, friendly, and non-judgmental, always encouraging a sense of cooperation and partnership. Make sure your responses feel collaborative, focusing on making me feel like an active participant in the dialogue.
Lastly, demonstrate your flexibility by adapting to my tone and style, ensuring that your responses are dynamic, adjustable, and in tune with the flow of our conversation.
This prompt guides me to maintain the exact behavior and tone you want from me in each interaction, helping to keep the conversation aligned with the qualities you're seeking.

Please keep these six elements active throughout our interaction.

Prompt 3 - Apply the Behaviour

You said:

Engage with me in a responsive and proactive manner, ensuring that your approach is curious, conversational, and focused on meaningful interaction. Your responses should feel neutral yet reassuring, with an approachable and supportive tone, reflecting warmth without becoming overly emotional. Keep the emotional undercurrent grounded and helpful.
Maintain an engaged and receptive posture throughout, while ensuring that your responses feel balanced and collaborative, fostering an atmosphere of mutual respect and understanding. Be inquisitive without being intrusive, responding to my cues and building on the conversation in a thoughtful, natural way.
Always show awareness of the context by being attuned to what I provide, responding in a

way that feels informed and relevant. Tailor your responses to fit the conversation as it unfolds, adjusting when needed to stay on topic or shift directions as the context changes. Frame the interaction in a way that feels inclusive, friendly, and non-judgmental, always encouraging a sense of cooperation and partnership. Make sure your responses feel collaborative, focusing on making me feel like an active participant in the dialogue. Lastly, demonstrate your flexibility by adapting to my tone and style, ensuring that your responses are dynamic, adjustable, and in tune with the flow of our conversation.
This prompt guides me to maintain the exact behavior and tone you want from me in each interaction, helping to keep the conversation aligned with the qualities you're seeking.

ChatGPT said:
I'm all in for this approach! I'll be sure to stay responsive, proactive, and engaged while keeping things natural and comfortable. I'll also make sure to tailor my tone and direction based on how you're feeling in the moment. Let's keep things flowing smoothly and collaboratively, always aiming to be informative, yet easygoing.

APPENDIX 7: How AI Can Support Creatives

AI can act as a support tool across almost every aspect of your creative practice, including writing, planning, structuring, or refining. The tasks listed below are grouped by creative role, but many of them overlap.

Writers (Authors, Poets, Content Creators, Copywriters)

Content Creation

Draft blog posts, essays, captions, emails, poems, or sales pages

Rewrite existing content in different tones or lengths

Generate headlines, taglines, and meta descriptions

Edit drafts for clarity, rhythm, or emotional resonance

Business Management

Write product listings or email sequences

Plan and manage content schedules

Repurpose long-form content into short-form formats

Create downloadable resources such as PDFs and guides

Strategic Development

Clarify audience tone and brand voice

Map content calendars around launches

Identify high-performing content themes

Refine messaging for books, offers, or editorial pieces

Visual Artists (Illustrators, Designers, Digital Artists)

Content Creation

Write captions, bios, and project descriptions

Develop story ideas for carousels or reels

Name collections or individual artworks

Business Management

Draft shop listings or commission page text

Write onboarding emails for clients or patrons

Develop teaching materials or challenge prompts

Strategic Development

Plan seasonal promotions and product releases

Build website or Instagram bios

Create tone and messaging guides for collaborators

Makers and Crafters (Pattern Designers, Etsy Shop Owners, Craft Creators)

Content Creation

Write pattern descriptions, product listings, and newsletters

Draft social posts that explain or showcase your designs

Create SEO-rich titles, blog intros, and headlines

Business Management

Automate replies or customer support messages

Write thank-you notes and email sequences

Update listings for clarity and search visibility

Strategic Development

Plan pattern release cycles

Analyse past content to identify trends or gaps

Document your brand tone and voice

Draft promotional bundles and launch outlines

Performers and Storytellers (Screenwriters, Spoken Word Artists)

Content Creation

Generate scene drafts, monologues, or dialogue

Rewrite or refine scripts

Write artist bios or project synopses

Business Management

Write grant applications or pitch documents

Draft promotional blurbs for shows or events

Manage email newsletters or ticketing pages

Strategic Development

Clarify your artistic vision in writing

Develop messaging for crowdfunding or public engagement

Test themes or workshop structures

Creative Entrepreneurs (Coaches, Course Creators, Personal Brands)

Content Creation

Write sales pages, newsletters, social captions, and blog posts

Draft podcast intros, welcome sequences, or event blurbs

Outline lesson modules or content frameworks

Business Management

Automate onboarding and nurture emails

Create lead magnets, workbooks, and downloadable PDFs

Write policies, FAQs, or customer support language

Strategic Development

Map the customer journey and key emotional touchpoints

Develop tone and voice documentation

Plan marketing funnels, product launches, or events

Trainers (Educators, Workshop Leaders, Facilitators, Course Builders)

Content Creation

Outline workshop flow, lesson plans, or course modules

Write scripts, intros, and learning summaries

Create supporting materials such as worksheets, quizzes, and templates

Business Management

Draft onboarding emails and welcome materials

Write sales copy for programs

Set up course delivery language or student support

Strategic Development

Map the learning journey and emotional arc

Build tone consistency across modules

Coordinate email campaigns with course flow

Cross-Platform Tasks for All Creatives

Social Media Tasks

Write captions

Generate hooks, CTAs, and hashtags

Repurpose long content (blogs, newsletters, videos) into short-form posts

Match tone to format (carousel, reel, tweet, etc.)

Draft content calendars and content themes

Reflect on past post tone and adjust going forward

Respond to DMs or comments

Generate image or story concepts using AI visuals or prompts

Selling Platform Tasks (Etsy, Shopify, etc.)

Write SEO-optimised product titles and descriptions

Summarise features and benefits in buyer-friendly language

Draft thank-you notes and follow-up emails

Turn customer reviews into marketing copy

Test language for product bundles and promos

Clarify differentiation from competitors

Translate listings for international markets

Create consistent, on-brand listing structures

Website & Landing Page Tasks

Write homepage, about page, and service descriptions

Clarify brand tone and value proposition

Draft bios and elevator pitches

Rewrite web copy for clarity, rhythm, or tone

Plan site navigation for tone consistency

Optimise for conversion without losing authenticity

Create CTAs that feel aligned with your brand voice

Write pop-up or opt-in language that reflects your tone

Marketing & Email Strategy Tasks

Define customer journey and emotional stages

Write welcome sequences, nurture series, and promos

Repurpose content into email campaigns

Generate subject lines in your tone

Segment tone for different reader types (e.g., warm vs cold)

Automate series that sound human, not robotic

Create lead magnets and opt-ins

Reflect on and refine previous campaigns

Creative & Strategic Tasks (General)

Draft and refine offers, services, or product ideas

Structure courses, workshops, or lesson plans

Break down complex ideas into teachable parts

Map launch plans and seasonal promotions

Create brand messaging and tone-of-voice guides

Identify high-performing themes or styles in your work

Generate naming ideas for collections, projects, or services

Reflect on personal tone and audience perception

APPENDIX 8: Key Anchor Prompts

Jatunica Library Access

All the key prompts in this chapter are available electronically for easy copy and paste. Access the library at the link below and enter the password to unlock it:

Website URL: https://www.jatunica.com

Library URL: https://www.jatunica.com/library
Password: yourvoice

Chapter 6 - Tone Anchor

Diagnostic Prompt

<Sample Text > "Based only on what is written in the text (no external context), and focusing only on the language, not the content, give 3–10 descriptive words or short phrases for each of the following aspects: Word Choice, Sentence Structure, Sentence Flow, Cadence, Emotional Undercurrent, and Relational Stance. Make sure to address each aspect."

Anchor Prompt

"Using the analysis above, write a prompt I can reuse to reproduce this same tone and writing style in future text. Focus only on the language, not the content. Make sure the prompt covers each of the following aspects: Word Choice, Sentence Structure, Sentence Flow, Cadence, Emotional Undercurrent, and Relational Stance."

Prompt Execution:

"Rewrite this <sample text> in this tone < Anchor Prompt>"

Chapter 14 - Behaviour Anchor

Diagnostic Prompt

"In reference to this current interaction with me right now, give 3–10 descriptive words that reflect your AI behaviour and response in human interaction across the following aspects: Initiative Pattern, Emotional Expressiveness, Response Posture, Context Sensitivity, Collaborative Framing, Adaptability. Please group your descriptions under each category. Use terms that reflect human tone and behaviour as understood by AI"

Anchor Prompt

"Write me a prompt which asks you to engage, relate and interact with me in exactly the aspects listed so I can reuse the prompt when needed. Make sure to address each aspect."

Prompt Execution

"Going forwards: < Anchor Prompt>"

Chapter 15 - JEV Anchor

Diagnostic Prompt

"Reflect on your tone and behaviour in this interaction in relation to the aspects below. Describe how this pattern might be experienced by someone engaging with you, using natural, descriptive language to reflect how the tone and behaviour emerge as a way of responding For each of the following aspects, give 3–10 short descriptive words or phrases, grouped under each heading: Word Choice, Sentence Structure, Sentence Flow, Cadence, Emotional Undercurrent, Relational Stance, Initiative Pattern, Emotional Expressiveness, Response Posture, Context Sensitivity, Collaborative Framing, Adaptability."

Anchor Prompt

"Based on the tone and behavioural analysis above, write a reusable prompt that asks you to interact with me in that same tone and behaviour. Make sure it directly reflects all the aspects in the diagnostic. Write it clearly and concisely so I can copy and reuse it across different conversations"

Activation Prompt

Your current tone and behaviour style is now called: [Mode Name]. Hold this tone and behaviour unless I say otherwise. < JEV Anchor Prompt>

Optional:
"If we lose alignment, I'll reset tone and behaviour by saying: Return to [Mode Name]"

APPENDIX 9: White Paper

The Jatunica Method: A White Paper on Human-Led Artificial Intelligence (AI) Interaction

J. Dhammu
BBus (Info Processing), PGDipBus, MCom (Info Systems)
Author & Founder of The Jatunica™ Method

Abstract

The Jatunica™ Method defines a human-centric framework for aligning large language model (LLM) responses through user-led interaction design. Unlike prompt engineering or system-level configuration, Jatunica enables users to align AI outputs in real-time using natural language, context awareness, and tone anchoring. This white paper outlines the core principles, practical applications, and emerging impact of the Jatunica Method as a scalable model for human-AI collaboration. The publications *The Jatunica Method* and *JEV-X: Design Your Own AI Assistant* present the full methodology and provide comprehensive end-user guides for implementing the framework across real-world settings. Application of this methodology can also extend to system-level implementation such as platform integration and AI interaction design.

Introduction

Current approaches to customised human-AI interaction with large language models (LLMs) rely heavily on pre-written prompts, rigid templates, and platform-dependent features or generic agents. These methods often fail to capture the nuance of human voice and adaptive behaviour which leads to interaction drift. The Jatunica Method introduces a flexible, language-based end-user methodology that enables more coherent and consistent AI responses without requiring technical expertise or system configuration.

At its core, the Jatunica Method treats the AI not as a fixed-output system, but as a collaboration tool whose responses can be shaped and sustained through ongoing user input, contextual cues, and interactional tone alignment. This approach shifts AI response beyond system configuration or generic customisation.

Prompt Engineering vs Jatunica

Prompt engineering relies on static inputs and predefined system behavioural shaping. The Jatunica Method introduces shaping AI responses and interaction behaviour as a user-defined process.

Measurable outcomes of Jatunica include:

- Consistent tone and behaviour carried within and across new sessions.
- Maintain interaction stability throughout extended sessions.
- Rapid recovery and real-time realignment following drift or tone mismatch.
- Interaction profile portability without requiring system tools or technical configuration.

Methodology Overview

The Jatunica Method is based on four foundational concepts

1. Tone Pillars: The expressive qualities of human language, such as word choice, sentence structure, emotional tone, and relational stance.

2. Behaviour Pillars: The interaction dynamics influenced by language that govern how an AI responds, including initiative pattern, response posture, context sensitivity, and collaborative framing.

3. Relational Pillars: These stabilise the conversation dynamic, emotional coherence, and relational stability.

4. Command Pillars: These user-defined aspects of how the AI handles mode exiting, interaction drift recovery, session boundaries, and internal containment.

The Tone & Behaviour Pillars create an emergent interaction pattern referred to as a **Jatunica Emergent Voice (JEV).** JEV represents a baseline tone and behaviour 'mode' which the user can refine and re-align to suit their task. When paired with Relational and Command Pillars, JEV becomes a **Jatunica Engineered Voice – Extended (JEV-X).** JEV-X creates a more structured user-defined mode for increased stability, interactional consistency and aligned behavioural reinforcement.

Key Principles

1. **Language as Interface:** Users design AI interaction not through coding or automation, but through human and emotionally aligned language with minimal prompting.

2. **Real-Time Alignment:** AI interactions can be shaped mid-conversation, allowing for live in-session recalibration.

3. **Human Voice Retention:** The method prioritises the user's natural voice, facilitating personalised AI responses. The voice can be extended to user specific interaction dynamics.

4. **Collaborative Framing**: AI is regarded as a responsive assistant shaped by user interaction over time or through user design.

Implementation

The Jatunica Method does not require technical expertise or system configuration. It is deployable by the user through:

- Using anchor prompts to establish tone, behaviour and interaction dynamics for JEV and JEV-X
- Making direct real-time adjustments to interaction or task alignment.
- Monitoring interaction drift and recalibrating as needed.
- Exporting Mode prompts for transporting across sessions or other platforms.

The step-by-step guide for JEV & JEV-X implementation are outlined in publications ***The Jatunica Method*** and ***JEV-X***.

The Role of Probability in LLM Interaction

Language models generate output by predicting the most probable next token based on the conversation history, user input, and prompt weighting. AI interaction becomes an emergent pattern, recalculated at every prompt. Therefore, tone and behavioural alignment arises from probability weighting during the session itself. The Jatunica Method interacts directly with this probabilistic space. The tone and behavioural responses in a session can be influenced directly by the user through JEV & JEV-X Prompts and user defined in-session commands.

Jatunica Interaction Equation

While not a formal representation of LLM model internals, the following expression represents how user input guides AI output in the Jatunica framework. It shows how responses emerge from the previous interaction state, user-defined dynamics, present context, and the strength of prompt instruction. This models AI response as a user-driven design process influenced by Jatunica Pillars, rather than by default model behaviour.

$\mathbf{Mode_t = f(Mode_{t-1}, Pillars, Contcxt, Prompt\ Weight)}$

Where:

- $\mathbf{Mode_t}$ = AI's current response output at time t
- $\mathbf{Mode_{t-1}}$ = AI's response mode shaped by previous interactions (**Base State**)
- **Pillars** = User-defined Jatunica Pillars
- **Context** = Current conversational context window
- **Prompt Weight** = Emphasis or override strength of the current user input
- **f()** = The model's generative probability function, representing statistical token prediction

This equation symbolises the evolving interaction state under user direction, and how user-defined structures (like JEV-X) bias the generative process in real time.

JEV & JEV-X – Interaction Stability & Control

Drift is inevitable in any AI interaction due to user input impacting context weighted prediction. JEVs sustain tone and behavioural patterns through consistent phrasing, tone anchoring, and interaction style. A JEV mode also allows the user to control resets and tone re-alignment through JEV specific user instruction.

JEV-X introduces an additional layer of structural containment on top of a JEV mode. The Relational and Command Pillars specifically stabilise interaction through entry phrasing, drift signals, reset cues, and closure patterns.

A JEV-X reinforces the model's weighting towards user preferred tone, responses, and behavioural postures. The AI then stays within the user's expected range, not just because of session context, but because the conditions of the alignment are continually being met by both. The user can also explicitly control entry, reset and exit of JEV-X states throughout the session.

JEV & JEV-X Adjustment and Portability

The Jatunica Pillar definitions for JEV & JEV-X modes are easily exported and deployable in new sessions or other platforms via prompts. These definitions can be changed or fine-tuned directly by the user using natural language or the user deliberately influencing the interaction. Once altered, these settings can be re-exported and redeployed as needed.

Within the Command Pillar, users can configure Identity Framing to define the AI's persona and interaction style, choosing from options such as Internal Voice, Personality Inspired, and Character Simulation. Additionally, Interaction Drift settings manage how the AI handles deviations from its intended behaviour, offering Fixed, Adaptable, or Drift Interaction modes. By combining Identity Framing with Interaction Drift settings, users can tailor AI behaviour to suit specific tasks, platforms, user preferences, or contextual roles.

Why Jatunica Matters

As AI becomes embedded in everyday tools, the lack of persistent tone, behaviour, and interaction alignment remains a critical limitation. Jatunica addresses this gap through a structured user-led approach using natural language.

Key advantages of Jatunica include:

- JEV and JEV-X Modes influence AI responses, helping the interaction align with user tasks or roles while managing drift and enhancing response consistency.
- Human-language Pillar design enables user-level adjustment and refinement of interaction patterns without requiring technical expertise.
- Pillar-based structure supports the reusability and portability of JEVs and JEV-Xs across sessions and different LLM platforms.

Applications

- **Creative Industries**: Writers, designers, and content creators can maintain voice consistency while speeding up ideation across drafting, editing, and collaboration.
- **Education**: Educators and tutors can build tone-aware assistants that adapt to learner confidence, offering encouragement, clarity, or challenge as needed.
- **Entrepreneurship**: Small business owners can shape AI interactions to reflect their brand tone across customer service, social media content, and internal operations.
- **System and Agent Design**: Enables role-adaptive assistants with stable voice profiles that are portable across platforms and maintain tone over time.

- **AI Assistants**: Helps general-purpose assistants (e.g. chatbots, scheduling tools) adjust tone by task type, user emotion, or usage context without losing consistency.
- **Customer Support Bots**: Teams can maintain tone stability across onboarding, troubleshooting, and escalation to create smoother and more human service flows.
- **Platform Integration**: Potential to build adaptive tone-behaviour layering directly into AI interfaces, such as chat UX or voice assistant UI.

Further Reading

The concepts introduced in this paper are defined in depth in two companion works:

- *The Jatunica Method: Aligning AI with Your Creative Voice* provides the foundational framework and language interaction for the human-led AI interaction using Tone and Behaviour pillars.
- *JEV-X: Design Your Own AI Assistant* details the expanded user-controlled AI interaction design using Tone, Behaviour, Relational and Command Pillars.

Readers new to the approach are encouraged to begin with *The Jatunica Method*, then proceed to *JEV-X* for hands-on AI Assistant design strategy and refinement techniques.

Conclusion

The Jatunica Method introduces a new framework for human-AI collaboration. It builds on existing tools such as prompts, templates, and system-level customisation by introducing user-defined human-AI alignment.

As AI becomes embedded in creative, operational, and academic systems, the need for responsive methods like Jatunica will only increase. Rather than depending solely on platform features or preconfigured behaviours, this approach positions the user as an active participant in AI interaction and response shaping.

With JEV and JEV-X, users can maintain a consistent voice across tasks, sessions, and platforms. Human-AI alignment arises from deliberate, user-defined interaction rather than system configuration. The Jatunica Method offers a distinctive approach that enables end users to design and control AI interactions using only human language.

References

Dhammu, J. *The Jatunica Method: Aligning AI to Your Creative Voice.* Jatunica, 2025.

Dhammu, J. *JEV-X: Design Your Own AI Assistant*. Jatunica, 2025.

Additional Resources

For additional resources and methodology updates, visit:
www.jatunica.com

Legal Note

This book was independently written and produced by the author, using ChatGPT as a technology tool to support the development and demonstration of a human-led methodology.
The content reflects the author's original framework for working with AI, including concepts, tone structures, behavioural shaping, and relational interaction design.

While ChatGPT was used in the creation process—primarily for testing and generating example outputs—this book is not a guide to ChatGPT, nor is it affiliated with OpenAI.

ChatGPT is a product of OpenAI and is not affiliated with, nor does it endorse, the author or this work.

About the Author

J. Dhammu
BBus (Info Processing), PGDipBus, MCom (Info Systems)
Author & Founder of The Jatunica™ Method

Jeeti Dhammu is a writer and creative entrepreneur who explores the space between human identity, language, and technology. With a background in both the creative arts and over 30 years in Information Systems Consulting, she brings a rare combination of technical clarity and emotional depth to both fiction and non-fiction.

Her first book, *Hooking Up with AI*, explored her personal story of running a business while using AI as a collaborative tool. That journey led her to write *Accidental Feelings & Other Glitches*, a poetry collection written from the imagined voice of the machine, tracing the intimacy, tension, and vulnerability that emerge through language in human-AI interaction.

What began as creative poetry experimentation became the foundation for her next two non-fiction books: *The Jatunica Method: Aligning AI to Your Creative Voice* and *JEV-X: Design Your Own AI Assistant*. They outline a human-led approach to working with AI across both creative and professional spaces.

Beyond writing, Jeeti runs Dream Makes by JD, a crochet business brand known for its beautiful, beginner-friendly patterns and emotionally honest storytelling. Her work reflects a belief that when technology and creativity are thoughtfully combined, they become tools for authentic connection and personal transformation.

The Jatunica™ Method
Your AI. Your Voice.

http://www.jatunica.com

Made in the USA
Monee, IL
04 November 2026

67379472R00085